NICHOLAS II

NICHOLAS II

George Vogt

CHELSEA HOUSE PUBLISHERS
NEW YORK
NEW HAVEN   PHILADELPHIA

EDITORIAL DIRECTOR: Nancy Toff
MANAGING EDITOR: Karyn Gullen Browne
COPY CHIEF: Perry Scott King
ART DIRECTOR: Giannella Garrett
ASSISTANT ART DIRECTOR: Carol McDougall
PICTURE EDITOR: Elizabeth Terhune

Staff for NICHOLAS II:

SENIOR EDITOR: John W. Selfridge
ASSISTANT EDITORS: Maria Behan, Pierre Hauser, Howard Ratner, Bert Yaeger
COPY EDITORS: Sean Dolan, Kathleen McDermott
ASSISTANT DESIGNER: Noreen Lamb
PICTURE RESEARCH: Ian Ensign
LAYOUT: Irene Friedman
PRODUCTION COORDINATOR: Alma Rodriguez
PRODUCTION ASSISTANT: Karen Dreste
COVER ILLUSTRATION: Richard Leonard

CREATIVE DIRECTOR: Harold Steinberg

Frontispiece courtesy of The Bettmann Archive

3 5 7 9 8 6 4 2

Library of Congress Cataloging in Publication Data

Vogt, George. NICHOLAS II

(World leaders past & present)
Bibliography: p.
Includes index.
1. Nicholas II, Emperor of Russia, 1868–1918—Juvenile
literature. 2. Soviet Union—Kings and rulers—Biography—
Juvenile literature. 3. Soviet Union—Politics and
government—1894–1917—Juvenile literature. I. Title.
II. Series.
DK258.V6   1987   947.08'3'0924   86-24469

ISBN 0-87754-545-6

Contents

ADENAUER
ALEXANDER THE GREAT
MARC ANTONY
KING ARTHUR
ATATÜRK
ATTLEE
BEGIN
BEN-GURION
BISMARCK
LÉON BLUM
BOLÍVAR
CESARE BORGIA
BRANDT
BREZHNEV
CAESAR
CALVIN
CASTRO
CATHERINE THE GREAT
CHARLEMAGNE
CHIANG KAI-SHEK
CHURCHILL
CLEMENCEAU
CLEOPATRA
CORTÉS
CROMWELL
DANTON
DE GAULLE
DE VALERA
DISRAELI
EISENHOWER
ELEANOR OF AQUITAINE
QUEEN ELIZABETH I
FERDINAND AND ISABELLA
FRANCO

FREDERICK THE GREAT
INDIRA GANDHI
MOHANDAS GANDHI
GARIBALDI
GENGHIS KHAN
GLADSTONE
GORBACHEV
HAMMARSKJÖLD
HENRY VIII
HENRY OF NAVARRE
HINDENBURG
HITLER
HO CHI MINH
HUSSEIN
IVAN THE TERRIBLE
ANDREW JACKSON
JEFFERSON
JOAN OF ARC
POPE JOHN XXIII
LYNDON JOHNSON
JUÁREZ
JOHN F. KENNEDY
KENYATTA
KHOMEINI
KHRUSHCHEV
MARTIN LUTHER KING, JR.
KISSINGER
LENIN
LINCOLN
LLOYD GEORGE
LOUIS XIV
LUTHER
JUDAS MACCABEUS
MAO ZEDONG

MARY, QUEEN OF SCOTS
GOLDA MEIR
METTERNICH
MUSSOLINI
NAPOLEON
NASSER
NEHRU
NERO
NICHOLAS II
NIXON
NKRUMAH
PERICLES
PERÓN
QADDAFI
ROBESPIERRE
ELEANOR ROOSEVELT
FRANKLIN D. ROOSEVELT
THEODORE ROOSEVELT
SADAT
STALIN
SUN YAT-SEN
TAMERLANE
THATCHER
TITO
TROTSKY
TRUDEAU
TRUMAN
VICTORIA
WASHINGTON
WEIZMANN
WOODROW WILSON
XERXES
ZHOU ENLAI

ON LEADERSHIP
Arthur M. Schlesinger, jr.

LEADERSHIP, it may be said, is really what makes the world go round. Love no doubt smooths the passage; but love is a private transaction between consenting adults. Leadership is a public transaction with history. The idea of leadership affirms the capacity of individuals to move, inspire, and mobilize masses of people so that they act together in pursuit of an end. Sometimes leadership serves good purposes, sometimes bad; but whether the end is benign or evil, great leaders are those men and women who leave their personal stamp on history.

Now, the very concept of leadership implies the proposition that individuals can make a difference. This proposition has never been universally accepted. From classical times to the present day, eminent thinkers have regarded individuals as no more than the agents and pawns of larger forces, whether the gods and goddesses of the ancient world or, in the modern era, race, class, nation, the dialectic, the will of the people, the spirit of the times, history itself. Against such forces, the individual dwindles into insignificance.

So contends the thesis of historical determinism. Tolstoy's great novel *War and Peace* offers a famous statement of the case. Why, Tolstoy asked, did millions of men in the Napoleonic wars, denying their human feelings and their common sense, move back and forth across Europe slaughtering their fellows? "The war," Tolstoy answered, "was bound to happen simply because it was bound to happen." All prior history predetermined it. As for leaders, they, Tolstoy said, "are but the labels that serve to give a name to an end and, like labels, they have the least possible connection with the event." The greater the leader, "the more conspicuous the inevitability and the predestination of every act he commits." The leader, said Tolstoy, is "the slave of history."

Determinism takes many forms. Marxism is the determinism of class. Nazism the determinism of race. But the idea of men and women as the slaves of history runs athwart the deepest human instincts. Rigid determinism abolishes the idea of human freedom—

the assumption of free choice that underlies every move we make, every word we speak, every thought we think. It abolishes the idea of human responsibility, since it is manifestly unfair to reward or punish people for actions that are by definition beyond their control. No one can live consistently by any deterministic creed. The Marxist states prove this themselves by their extreme susceptibility to the cult of leadership.

More than that, history refutes the idea that individuals make no difference. In December 1931 a British politician crossing Park Avenue in New York City between 76th and 77th Streets around 10:30 P.M. looked in the wrong direction and was knocked down by an automobile—a moment, he later recalled, of a man aghast, a world aglare: "I do not understand why I was not broken like an eggshell or squashed like a gooseberry." Fourteen months later an American politician, sitting in an open car in Miami, Florida, was fired on by an assassin; the man beside him was hit. Those who believe that individuals make no difference to history might well ponder whether the next two decades would have been the same had Mario Constasino's car killed Winston Churchill in 1931 and Giuseppe Zangara's bullet killed Franklin Roosevelt in 1933. Suppose, in addition, that Adolf Hitler had been killed in the street fighting during the Munich *Putsch* of 1923 and that Lenin had died of typhus during World War I. What would the 20th century be like now?

For better or for worse, individuals do make a difference. "The notion that a people can run itself and its affairs anonymously," wrote the philosopher William James, "is now well known to be the silliest of absurdities. Mankind does nothing save through initiatives on the part of inventors, great or small, and imitation by the rest of us—these are the sole factors in human progress. Individuals of genius show the way, and set the patterns, which common people then adopt and follow."

Leadership, James suggests, means leadership in thought as well as in action. In the long run, leaders in thought may well make the greater difference to the world. But, as Woodrow Wilson once said, "Those only are leaders of men, in the general eye, who lead in action. . . . It is at their hands that new thought gets its translation into the crude language of deeds." Leaders in thought often invent in solitude and obscurity, leaving to later generations the tasks of imitation. Leaders in action—the leaders portrayed in this series—have to be effective in their own time.

And they cannot be effective by themselves. They must act in response to the rhythms of their age. Their genius must be adapted, in a phrase of William James's, "to the receptivities of the moment." Leaders are useless without followers. "There goes the mob," said the French politician hearing a clamor in the streets. "I am their leader. I must follow them." Great leaders turn the inchoate emotions of the mob to purposes of their own. They seize on the opportunities of their time, the hopes, fears, frustrations, crises, potentialities. They succeed when events have prepared the way for them, when the community is awaiting to be aroused, when they can provide the clarifying and organizing ideas. Leadership ignites the circuit between the individual and the mass and thereby alters history.

It may alter history for better or for worse. Leaders have been responsible for the most extravagant follies and most monstrous crimes that have beset suffering humanity. They have also been vital in such gains as humanity has made in individual freedom, religious and racial tolerance, social justice and respect for human rights.

There is no sure way to tell in advance who is going to lead for good and who for evil. But a glance at the gallery of men and women in *World Leaders—Past and Present* suggests some useful tests.

One test is this: do leaders lead by force or by persuasion? By command or by consent? Through most of history leadership was exercised by the divine right of authority. The duty of followers was to defer and to obey. "Theirs not to reason why,/ Theirs but to do and die." On occasion, as with the so-called "enlightened despots" of the 18th century in Europe, absolutist leadership was animated by humane purposes. More often, absolutism nourished the passion for domination, land, gold and conquest and resulted in tyranny.

The great revolution of modern times has been the revolution of equality. The idea that all people should be equal in their legal condition has undermined the old structure of authority, hierarchy and deference. The revolution of equality has had two contrary effects on the nature of leadership. For equality, as Alexis de Tocqueville pointed out in his great study *Democracy in America*, might mean equality in servitude as well as equality in freedom.

"I know of only two methods of establishing equality in the political world," Tocqueville wrote. "Rights must be given to every citizen, or none at all to anyone . . . save one, who is the master of all." There was no middle ground "between the sovereignty of all and the absolute power of one man." In his astonishing prediction of 20th-century totalitarian dictatorship, Tocqueville explained how the revolution of equality could lead to the *"Führerprinzip"* and more terrible absolutism than the world had ever known.

But when rights are given to every citizen and the sovereignty of all is established, the problem of leadership takes a new form, becomes more exacting than ever before. It is easy to issue commands and enforce them by the rope and the stake, the concentration camp and the *gulag.* It is much harder to use argument and achievement to overcome opposition and win consent. The Founding Fathers of the United States understood the difficulty. They believed that history had given them the opportunity to decide, as Alexander Hamilton wrote in the first Federalist Paper, whether men are indeed capable of basing government on "reflection and choice, or whether they are forever destined to depend . . . on accident and force."

Government by reflection and choice called for a new style of leadership and a new quality of followership. It required leaders to be responsive to popular concerns, and it required followers to be active and informed participants in the process. Democracy does not eliminate emotion from politics; sometimes it fosters demagoguery; but it is confident that, as the greatest of democratic leaders put it, you cannot fool all of the people all of the time. It measures leadership by results and retires those who overreach or falter or fail.

It is true that in the long run despots are measured by results too. But they can postpone the day of judgment, sometimes indefinitely, and in the meantime they can do infinite harm. It is also true that democracy is no guarantee of virtue and intelligence in government, for the voice of the people is not necessarily the voice of God. But democracy, by assuring the right of opposition, offers built-in resistance to the evils inherent in absolutism. As the theologian Reinhold Niebuhr summed it up, "Man's capacity for justice makes democracy possible, but man's inclination to injustice makes democracy necessary."

A second test for leadership is the end for which power is sought. When leaders have as their goal the supremacy of a master race or the promotion of totalitarian revolution or the acquisition and exploitation of colonies or the protection of greed and privilege or the preservation of personal power, it is likely that their leadership will do little to advance the cause of humanity. When their goal is the abolition of slavery, the liberation of women, the enlargement of opportunity for the poor and powerless, the extension of equal rights to racial minorities, the defense of the freedoms of expression and opposition, it is likely that their leadership will increase the sum of human liberty and welfare.

Leaders have done great harm to the world. They have also conferred great benefits. You will find both sorts in this series. Even "good" leaders must be regarded with a certain wariness. Leaders are not demigods; they put on their trousers one leg after another just like ordinary mortals. No leader is infallible, and every leader needs to be reminded of this at regular intervals. Irreverence irritates leaders but is their salvation. Unquestioning submission corrupts leaders and demands followers. Making a cult of a leader is always a mistake. Fortunately hero worship generates its own antidote. "Every hero," said Emerson, "becomes a bore at last."

The signal benefit the great leaders confer is to embolden the rest of us to live according to our own best selves, to be active, insistent, and resolute in affirming our own sense of things. For great leaders attest to the reality of human freedom against the supposed inevitabilities of history. And they attest to the wisdom and power that may lie within the most unlikely of us, which is why Abraham Lincoln remains the supreme example of great leadership. A great leader, said Emerson, exhibits new possibilities to all humanity. "We feed on genius. . . . Great men exist that there may be greater men."

Great leaders, in short, justify themselves by emancipating and empowering their followers. So humanity struggles to master its destiny, remembering with Alexis de Tocqueville: "It is true that around every man a fatal circle is traced beyond which he cannot pass; but within the wide verge of that circle he is powerful and free; as it is with man, so with communities."

—*New York*

1

The New Tsar

The tsar's funeral procession seemed 2,000 miles long. From Sevastopol on the Black Sea, along the Dnieper River and through the cities and towns of the Ukraine and central Russian highlands, past crowds of tearful subjects lining the railway, toward the old capital of Moscow and the new capital of St. Petersburg steamed the train bearing the body of Tsar Alexander III. The outpouring of public emotion was testimony to the awe and respect accorded the dead emperor. Inside the train, numb with grief and weighed down by the sudden transfer of responsibility to his shoulders, rode Nicholas II, Alexander's son and the new tsar.

Many times during the trip, Nicholas must have reflected on the radical change that had come over his life so quickly. Barely six months before, the heir to the throne had been in the midst of a carefree, whirlwind tour of Europe, visiting royal relatives in England and, more enjoyable, courting Alix of Hesse-Darmstadt, the beautiful German princess and granddaughter of Queen Victoria of England. Nicholas returned to Russia 26 years old and deeply in love with his new fiancée, "Sunny."

What is going to happen to me . . . to all of Russia? I am not prepared to be a Tsar.
—NICHOLAS II

About six months before he ascended the throne in November 1894, Nicholas II had this portrait taken in London. He was there in the company of Queen Victoria, near the time of his 26th birthday, to celebrate his recent engagement to Princess Alix of Hesse-Darmstadt, Victoria's granddaughter.

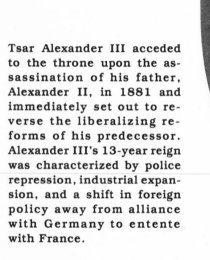

Tsar Alexander III acceded to the throne upon the assassination of his father, Alexander II, in 1881 and immediately set out to reverse the liberalizing reforms of his predecessor. Alexander III's 13-year reign was characterized by police repression, industrial expansion, and a shift in foreign policy away from alliance with Germany to entente with France.

There were few clouds on the horizon. Nicholas's father was a robust 49 years old, a born leader of men. He intended to rule as emperor for decades, only gradually training his son to succeed him. Six feet, four inches tall and bearlike in physique, Alexander dwarfed the five-foot, seven-inch "Nicky," and radiated power and authority over generals, ministers, subjects, and family alike. Nicholas, unlike his forebears in the 19th century, was heir at birth to the Russian throne. With the empire in good hands, Nicky and Sunny could look forward to a leisurely and privileged life, centering around family, friends, glittering social events, and long trips through Russia and Europe.

Alix married the new tsar Nicholas II in November 1894. To do so, the deeply religious princess was obliged to convert from Protestantism to Russian Orthodoxy, choosing the Russified name *Alexandra Fyodorovna* at her baptism.

Suddenly the imperial family's expectations for a brilliant social season in St. Petersburg, with a gala wedding as centerpiece, were shattered. The tsar became ill, at first not seriously, then enough to concern his family and ministers. As his condition steadily worsened, the family consulted a Viennese medical specialist, who diagnosed a serious kidney ailment. Ordered to bed for a complete rest, the patient at first was reluctant; he had an empire to run. Eventually, even Alexander realized that a change of scene and pace was necessary, so the entire family went south to Livadia, the tsar's spectacular palace on the Crimean peninsula. There, where the sunny climate and Black Sea breezes had helped cure so many Russian noblemen of tuberculosis and other diseases, the family waited anxiously.

One year before the awesome responsibility for governing the world's largest nation fell to Nicholas, he was given his first administrative task. Much to Alexander's surprise, a trusted adviser, Count Sergei Yulevich Witte, appointed Nicholas in 1893 to head a committee overseeing construction of the Trans-Siberian Railway. In his usual brusque fashion, Alexander demanded to know whether Witte knew how unsuited the immature tsar's son was for the job. The tsar thundered that, even at the age of 25, Nicholas was still a child.

For a few weeks, Alexander improved, but in late September the symptoms returned and his condition worsened. In desperation, the family turned to holy men and "miracle workers." Sensing disaster, Nicholas summoned Sunny to Livadia and immediately took her before the tsar for his formal blessing of their engagement. What they found was a pale, tired man who had bravely struggled into full military uniform in their honor. Alexander blessed them without rising, and 10 days later he died. At 2:30 P.M. on the afternoon of November 1, 1894, Nicky became Nicholas II, "Tsar and Autocrat of All the Russias," absolute ruler of the largest empire on earth. As the term "autocrat" in the tsar's title implies, this form of rulership gave all governing power to a single leader. The *narod* (the people or citizenry) would now be expected to look up to the young Nicholas as the one responsible for Russia's future. Grief stricken, the young emperor collapsed into the arms of his brother-in-law, sobbing, "What am I going to do? What is going to happen to me . . . to all of Russia? I am not prepared to be a Tsar. I never wanted to become one. I know nothing of the business of ruling."

The funeral train rolled north from the warm, sunlit Crimea (the peninsula that extends into the Black Sea) to the chilly, gray cities of Russia. Suddenly in charge of everything, Nicholas had difficulty in overcoming his sense of loss and taking command. In the days prior to leaving Livadia, Nicholas's most urgent problem had been to supervise

A peasant couple from the Lena River region of Siberia.
In 1861 Alexander II freed over 20 million serfs (peasants bound to their land) — who made up a large per-
centage of the population — from the oppression they had
suffered working for landlords. However, though half the
farmed land in Russia was turned over to the freed serfs,
they received the least productive fields.

complex arrangements for the state funeral. No tsar had ever gone to his grave without elaborate ceremony, and Alexander's death was greatly mourned. Preparations included the funeral train, major processions in Moscow and St. Petersburg, and the funeral itself. Military units for the parade as well as security had to be dispatched; courtiers, ministers, and church officials had to be instructed; foreign governments had to be notified and invited to send delegations; and royal relatives from all over Europe had to be housed and fed. Most troublesome of all, Nicholas had to cope with the large imperial family, which included numerous grand dukes and duchesses and their families, all of them very free with advice for their "Nicky."

It was too much for the young tsar. Some details went unattended; some orders went unissued. Upon arrival in St. Petersburg, the tsar discovered chaos. Even the weather presented difficulties. Whole groups of officials got lost in the drizzle, and others conversed and laughed loudly along the route of the procession. Superstitious peasants in the crowd found an evil omen in the German princess's

Red Square is the ceremonial focus of the Kremlin, the walled fortress that dominates Moscow. In 1896 Nicholas and Alexandra were formally crowned in the Kremlin, as was the custom for all Russian monarchs.

arrival in the capital behind the coffin. At the cathedral courtiers wrangled over the preferred places and best views. Because of the bungled planning, there were those who wryly suggested that Alexander should have made his own funeral arrangements: he, at least, would not have tolerated such incompetence and irreverence.

One week after the funeral, Nicholas married Alix before friends and family in a chapel of the Winter Palace. At this same palace a mere 13 years later, a government not commanded by a tsar would be overthrown in a coup that would decisively alter the course of Russian and world history.

At the time of Alexander's death, the couple had decided to wed without delay. In preparation Alix, a Lutheran, converted to the Russian Orthodox faith, the religion of the tsars. In keeping with tradition, she adopted a Russian name upon baptism into the church, thus becoming Alexandra Fyodorovna, the name she would use as tsarina for the rest of her life.

With marriage, a measure of calm returned to Nicholas's life. The imperial couple began married life in an apartment of the Anichkov Palace, under the watchful eye of Nicholas's mother, the Dowager Empress Maria Alexandrovna. Soon, to alleviate friction between Alexandra and her mother-in-law, the couple moved to a separate residence that Alexandra could make her own. The perfect spot proved to be the smaller of two palaces — only 100 rooms compared to more that 200 in the "big" palace — at Tsarskoe Selo, meaning "The Tsar's Village," just outside St. Petersburg. Nicholas and Alexandra energetically threw themselves into making the palace a home. Their first year together was spent largely in anticipation of their first child, a girl, and in preparation for the formal coronation ceremony and public celebrations to be held in the spring of 1896.

According to tradition, tsars and tsarinas were always crowned in elaborate religious ceremonies in the Uspensky Cathedral inside the walls of Moscow's ancient fortress, the Kremlin. Preceded by formal processions into the old capital and followed by days

Our marriage seemed to me a mere continuation of the masses for the dead, with this difference — that I now wore a white dress instead of a black one.
—ALEXANDRA
from a diary entry
describing her wedding
to Nicholas II

In accord with tradition, Nicholas crowned himself and then Alexandra with the same crown created in 1762 for the coronation of Catherine the Great. The crown, made of diamonds and pearls, weighs almost 4.5 pounds and incorporates at its top a spinel, or colored gem, originally bought for Tsar Alexei Mikhailovich in 1676 from Emperor Kang Hi of China.

of lavish banquets, public celebrations, and private parties, the coronation of a tsar was a rare opportunity for all layers of Russian society to celebrate at one time, though not necessarily together. Nicholas paid particular attention to the ordinary citizens, ordering enough free food and drink to feed thousands of his subjects.

The coronation itself was a grand spectacle. Nicholas and Alexandra, wearing heavy, jewel-encrusted coronation robes, walked down red-carpeted stairs into a cathedral ablaze with candles, their light reflected in jeweled screens, priceless gold religious icons, and fortunes in gems on almost every arm and neck. After receiving the traditional blessings of the church, Nicholas raised the spectacular imperial crown of Catherine the Great and, as custom demanded, crowned first himself and then his wife. One hundred and one cannon shots signaled the advent of a new tsar to the nation.

For days Moscow had groaned under the masses of people pouring into the city. Peasants eagerly sought to see and be near their "Little Father," as the tsars were called, and to celebrate with him and his beautiful bride. Having received widespread re-

Nicholas and Alexandra display their court robes in 1904. The opulent official dress still reflected the Eastern legacy that had been left by the Mongol domination of Russia from the mid-13th century to the late 1400s.

ports of free food and drink, conveyed by the newly expanded railway system, the crowds descended on Moscow in unprecedented numbers. Every available room and apartment was filled, and tens of thousands simply camped out in public places.

Khodynka Field (later to become the Moscow Central Airport), an enormous military training ground, was the focal point because it was there that the tsar's men would dispense food and beer. The night before, immense, happy hordes began moving through the streets of Moscow toward the field. Perhaps about half a million people succeeded in reaching the area, where their revels continued until dawn. Many more — the lucky ones — were unable to break through the crush and turned back.

In the early morning, the crowd's mood changed as rumors spread of food and beer shortages. A few people charged the roped-off food stands and others followed. Soon the entire field was a mass of churning, heaving bodies as wave upon wave pressed beyond the small force of soldiers assigned to maintain order. Unable to see around themselves, many people slipped and fell into trenches dug for training purposes and were trampled to death. Meanwhile, at the far end of the gigantic field, completely unaware of the unfolding tragedy, sat a large, elegantly dressed crowd of noblemen, merchants, and military officers listening to a special choral performance attended by the tsar and tsarina.

The toll was horrendous — at least 1,400 persons killed and many more injured. Other estimates say that as many as 3,000 persons might have been trampled to death. Very likely, these "official" estimates were deliberately low. With more than enough blame to go around, some fell on Nicholas himself, and some fell on Nicholas's uncle Sergei Alexandrovich — "Prince Khodynsky" as the tsar's family affectionately called him. He was governor general of Moscow and, therefore, the person in charge of controlling crowds. In what was surely one of the worst decisions of his short reign, Nicholas allowed the coronation balls and parties to continue even as Moscow was awash in blood and bodies. Though they attended memorial services, visited hospitals, and gave a thousand rubles to the family of each victim, the imperial couple could not escape the stain of Khodynka. Incredibly, only eight days after the tragedy, Nicholas was back again at Khodynka, this time presiding over a huge military review, the concluding event of the coronation festivities.

Whatever the toll in lives, the damage to the tsar's prestige was greater. As head of state, Nicholas suffered with every embarrassment to Russia. Foreign dignitaries were especially quick to criticize his failure to cancel the celebrations and to compare him unfavorably to his late father. But virtually nothing in Nicholas's 26 years had prepared him to make important decisions and exercise firm leadership. The long apprenticeship to his father had been denied him, so Nicholas began his reign with a series of blunders and embarrassments that more experienced men would have avoided. A chaotic funeral and then Khodynka — these events of Nicholas's first 19 months as tsar gave dark hints of greater disasters ahead.

Reading a Letter, a scene painted by I. M. Pryanishnikova at the end of the 19th century. Looking for someone to read her a letter she has received, a servant girl goes to a grocer's shop, where a government official obliges her. In this period only 12 percent of Russian women were literate.

2

Nicholas at Home

Two and a half centuries before the birth of Nicholas, the English ambassador to the Russian court ended a dispatch to his monarch, Queen Elizabeth I, with a rhyme:

Loe thus I make an Ende: none other news to thee
But that the country is too cold, the people
    beastly bee.

Had the ambassador returned in the 1890s, he would have found court life more to his liking, the country dramatically changed in size and shape, but the weather still the same.

Nicholas I, who ruled Russia from 1825 to 1855, had been known as the "Iron Tsar." No sooner had Nicholas I become tsar on December 26 than he was met with a revolt. Its leaders demanded constitutional restraints on the tsar's power. The Decembrists, as they were called, were defeated, and many were thrown into prison.

Through two brief wars, one with Persia (now Iran) from 1826 to 1828, and the other with Turkey, ending in 1829, Nicholas I gained territory for his already gigantic nation.

When a wave of revolutionary fervor swept

The Decembrists were crushed.
But the spark lived.
—HARRISON E. SALISBURY
American historian

Nicholas visits Paris on October 6, 1896. Tsar Alexander III had established a firm Franco-Russian alliance in the face of Germany's increasing military might. Nicholas, as tsar, would prove a less resolute and decisive ruler.

Alexander II, Nicholas's reform-minded grandfather, ruled from 1855 to 1881. In addition to freeing the serfs, he established self-governing bodies (*zemstvos*) at the local level, instituted the principle of equality before the law and the right to trial by jury, and required conscription into the army from all social classes.

through France and Germany in 1848, Nicholas I smashed all similar movements in Russia.

Although determined to carve out an empire for Russia in the Far East, which eventually led to the Crimean War with Great Britain and France, Nicholas I did not ignore domestic problems. He built schools and instituted laws intended to improve conditions for the serfs — the peasants owned as virtual slaves by landowners.

By the time Nicholas II was born, on May 18 (or May 6 according to the old Russian calendar), 1868, 400 years of wars, diplomacy, and imperial marriages had produced a patchwork country stretching 6,000 miles from central Poland in the west to the Bering Sea and Pacific Ocean in the east. North to south, the country extended more than 2,000 miles from the Arctic Ocean to the deserts north of present-day Iran and Afghanistan. By the 1890s the Russian empire covered one-sixth of the total land surface of the globe and included more than 125 million people.

Governing an empire of such size and diversity was a complicated matter. First, there were more than 100 different nationalities scattered across the land—Poles, Germans, Tatars, Uzbeks, Ukrainians, and Jews — most with their own languages, religions, and cultures. Second, geography and climate made the land remarkably unfriendly to settlement and development. Russia lies so far north that much of the country experiences bitterly cold winters, heavy snows, permanently frozen subsoils ("permafrost"), and short growing seasons. On the other hand, the southern portion of the country is a blazing desert. Wide rivers, icy swamps, dense forests, deserts, or inland seas make parts of the Soviet Union impassable and, to this day, complicate construction of railways, pipelines, and roads. In 1868 the easiest way to travel from St. Petersburg (known, since 1924, as Leningrad) in the west to Vladivostok in the east was to board a ship and sail halfway around the world.

Geography was not the only problem. The huge Russian government included the large imperial family; a vast, slow-moving bureaucracy; an overgrown, ill-equipped, poorly commanded military; and a council of ministers composed more often than not of wealthy conservatives from the upper levels of Russian society. There was no European-style parliament or elected assembly, and there was almost no check on the powers of the tsar. Suspicion and contempt for the West, democracy, and social change were prevalent among the Russian ruling classes.

Until the "Great Reforms" under Nicholas II's grandfather, Alexander II, there had been little movement toward social change and improved conditions for the poverty-stricken peasants, who composed the large majority of the population.

When the Russian army met defeat in the Crimean War (1853–56) against the technologically more advanced British and French forces, Alex-

[Tsar Alexander II] could not admit that reform had failed and that his regime was ingrained with terror, choking in bureaucracy, drowning in ignorance and greed. He grew more rigid, more cranky, more repressive, and now the deadly spiral spun faster and faster — more young men and women arrested; more violence against the state; more attempts at assassination; more assassinations; more arrests; more executions.
—HARRISON E. SALISBURY
American historian

ander quickly realized that Russia had to begin catching up with the times. He understood that the need for change meant more than simply to update the Russian military. Although there was no question that the tsar naturally would remain Russia's autocratic ruler, Alexander realized that modernizing his country meant making substantial social reforms. Serfdom, the harsh feudal system whereby landowners also owned the peasants who worked the land, Alexander II believed, would have to be done away with, and he warned of the dangers of rebellion if the government did not act responsibly to correct the injustice.

Many major Russian literary figures had criticized the institution of serfdom in their works. Most notably Alexander Pushkin, considered by many to be Russia's greatest poet, was sent away from St. Petersburg by Alexander I after the tsar became impatient with Pushkin's verses against serfdom.

The interior of a typical 19th-century peasant house on display in a Moscow museum.

During the rule of Nicholas I, Russia's greatest writer was the comic and satirical genius Nikolai Gogol. In Gogol's novel *Dead Souls* his protagonist seeks wealth through a legal loophole that permits him to buy dead serfs who are regarded as alive until the next census is taken. The novelist Ivan Turgenev, who began his literary career shortly before Alexander II ascended the throne, held a post in the Ministry of Internal Affairs, an agency of the government then working to free the serfs.

On March 3, 1861, over the strong objections of the landowning nobility, Alexander II freed the serfs and began a program of dramatic reform. He abolished corporal punishment, restructured the judiciary and the educational system, and denied many of the privileges the nobility had enjoyed. In fact, the emancipation of the serfs brought financial hardship to many landowning families.

In 1881 young Nicholas's world erupted in violence and changed his life forever. Despite his liberal reforms, there were at least half a dozen attempts on Alexander II's life by different revolutionary groups. Impatient with Alexander's policies, these groups wished to overthrow the existing regime. For years, a group called the Will of the People had stalked the tsar. On March 13 Alexander's passing carriage was demolished by a bomb thrown from the sidewalk. Miraculously unhurt, he stepped from the debris to assist his injured servants only to be horribly wounded by a second bomb hurled between his legs. Carried to the palace, the tsar died in front of his hastily summoned family. In that moment, Nicholas's father became the tsar and Nicholas the heir to the throne or *tsarevich* (son of the tsar). The 12-year-old boy never forgot the sight of his grandfather's mangled body, one leg gone, the other in shreds, his chest torn open, and his face bloodied. Because he could not forgive the revolutionaries who had so brutally murdered his grandfather, Nicholas looked with contempt on Russia's radicals and those referred to as "leftists" who worked for the cause of rapid political change.

Young Nicholas grew up in a family deeply scarred by the violent act and dedicated to the eradication

THE BETTMANN ARCHIVE

An 1841 painting depicts the author Nikolai Gogol. His comic and satirical works earned him an important place among Russian writers in the mid-19th century. His greatest contributions included the elevation of realistic, satirical prose to a preeminent place in Russian literature and the introduction of peasants and clerks as protagonists.

Alexander II's reforms fell far short of satisfying those Russians who envied European political and social achievements. From their ranks came his assassins, a group called the Will of the People, which stalked him from 1879 until a bomb injured him fatally on March 13, 1881. As a boy of 12, a horrified Nicholas witnessed his grandfather's death after the attack.

THE BETTMANN ARCHIVE

of his grandfather's enemies. Under Alexander III, the full force of the government was turned on the revolutionaries and other "un-Russian" groups. To a remarkable degree, Nicholas's father succeeded in imprisoning his foes or driving them into exile in Europe. He was also partially successful in turning back the clock through a series of counterreforms intended to remedy Alexander II's "liberal" excesses. These included "temporary regulations" that gave authorities broad powers in dealing with the press and anyone capable of threatening public order. The regulations, amounting to a kind of martial law, were kept in force for the next 36 years.

Other extreme measures included the elimination of radical and liberal publications, tight controls over universities and student groups, more power for the conservative Russian Orthodox church over schools, and other measures designed to strengthen the aristocracy at the expense of peasants and villagers. Most important of all, Alexander III immediately canceled his father's plan to call for a representative assembly to advise on questions of reform, and he replaced many of the former tsar's ministers with men whose conservatism was not in doubt. One of the leading figures of this reactionary campaign was Constantine Pobedonostsev, a conservative legal scholar, whom Alexander named to be the lay (non-clerical) head of the Russian Orthodox church. For more than two decades, Pobedonostsev had labored with dedication to strengthen the autocracy (the tsar's personal and total power over all matters of government) and to make the Russian Orthodox church dominant.

The 13 years of Alexander III's reign saw an upsurge in pressure on minority religions, including organized massacres ("pogroms") of Jews, and an active and bitterly resented campaign to "Russify" the non-Russian peoples. The government attempted to force the adoption of the Russian language in schools and to stamp out evidence of non-Russian writings and culture. In effect, the tsar tried to make non-Russians adopt the religion, language, and culture of the Great Russians, who were the largest single national group but a minority within the empire. In areas such as Poland, the Ukraine, and the Caucasus region, these efforts were bitterly resented and resisted. Alexander did, however, afford the peasants a bank to help finance land ownership. But he revoked certain *zemstvo* laws providing limited local self-government that Alexander II had endorsed. This was in retaliation for his father's murder. A year after becoming tsar, Nicholas himself would dismiss zemstvo representatives' democratic ideas as "irrational dreams."

Nicholas's childhood was generally happy, though he and his two brothers and two sisters were raised under strict discipline and permitted few luxuries. The children's meals, for example, began only after the aloof and rigid Tsar Alexander decided to leave the table.

Although intelligent, reasonably well-educated, and well-traveled, young Nicholas was a prisoner of his wealth and social rank. He absorbed most of the extreme views of his conservative father and Constantine Pobedonostsev, who was Nicholas's tutor during childhood and served as his father's closest counselor. Like his father, Nicholas blamed much of the social agitation and violence on Russian Jews

Constantine Pobedonostsev served both Alexander III and Nicholas as tutor and adviser. His reactionary views in opposition to individual liberties and parliamentary government and in favor of religious orthodoxy and the untrammeled authority of the tsar reinforced both rulers' repressive tendencies.

31

and supported the brutal persecutions of a people he referred to with hatred as "Christ-killers." He viewed freedom of the press as a threat to autocracy and supported press censorship. He scorned representative assemblies and popular elections. Visiting France as a young man, Nicholas met with a group that included numerous French deputies from the National Assembly. He haughtily refused to speak to any who had not been appointed cabinet ministers by the head of state.

When he was old enough, Nicholas was named to the council of empire and to the committee of ministers. The young tsarevich often escaped from official responsibilities in the company of fellow officers whom he had met during his extensive military education under General Danilevsky. Nicholas was in the general's charge for 12 years. Another tutor, the Englishman Charles Heath, taught the tsarevich what became his astonishingly good English. As cadets, they attended parties and balls, played cards, rode horses, and behaved more or less like the other young men of high society. His mother occasionally urged him to "dance more and smoke less." In their company, Nicholas met and fell in love with a beautiful ballerina, Mathilde Kschessinska, who, as a commoner, could not hope to marry him. Despite the disapproval of his parents, Nicholas spent much time in Mathilde's company. Their love affair ended only when Nicholas met and fell in love with Princess Alix.

With his father's sudden death and his marriage to Princess Alix, Nicholas's life again changed dramatically. The Russian tsar, after all, was one of the wealthiest and most powerful men in the world. Nicholas might have preferred simple peasant blouses and trousers to court uniforms, but he still presided over the entire government of Russia and over vast personal estates. These included enormous tracts of farmland and forests that produced the tsar's huge annual income. From that, he was expected to maintain seven palaces, 15,000 imperial officials and servants, the imperial train and yacht, the staffs and companies of five imperial theaters, the Imperial Academy, and the Imperial Bal-

SOVFOTO

Michel Fokine and Tamara Karsavina dance a divertissement, "Fisherman and the Pearl," from *Zhavotta* at the Mariinsky Theater in St. Petersburg in 1902. Fokine and Karsavina were two of the most esteemed members of the ballet troupe under the patronage of the tsar. By this time Russian ballet had led the world for two decades.

Nicholas and Alexandra present their firstborn, Olga, to her great-grandmother Queen Victoria. Olga, the eldest of four daughters, was born in 1895.

let. In addition, he was expected to provide large annual allowances to the grand dukes and wedding dowries to the grand duchesses. Not surprisingly, the treasury was often empty by year's end.

But the glitter of court life and St. Petersburg society held little appeal for Nicholas and Alexandra. She spoke Russian with difficulty at first. Alexandra and Nicholas spoke and wrote to each other in English. She felt shy and awkward. Raised as a strict Lutheran (a member of the founding church of Protestant Christianity) in a quiet, uneventful German court, she was shocked by Russian society, its many love affairs and extravagant parties. Alexandra gradually withdrew from the St. Petersburg social scene and built a very private life for herself and her family in the Alexander Palace at Tsarskoe Selo. Her pregnancies were all difficult, and the long confinements also limited her contact with outsiders. Naturally, the grand dukes and duchesses resented this.

In the years between 1895 and 1901, cannons announced the birth of four imperial babies. Each time a new child was born the cannons stopped

Not until the birth of their fifth child in 1904 did Nicholas and Alexandra produce an heir to the throne, since Russian tradition did not allow a female to inherit the imperial mantle. Shown here are their children: from left to right, Tatiana, Maria, Anastasia, Olga, and the tsarevich, Alexis.

firing only after 101 salutes. The babies were all girls — Olga in 1895, Tatiana in 1897, Maria in 1899, and Anastasia in 1901 — and none could inherit the throne. Unless Alexandra produced a son, and the cannons sounded 300 times, the heir to the throne remained Nicholas's younger brother Mikhail.

As a parent, Nicholas encouraged a much warmer family atmosphere than he had experienced as a child, and he seemed to prefer his family duties to those of state. The imperial family enjoyed a grand and luxurious lifestyle. Each spring they boarded their private train for a trip to the Black Sea, where they spent a few months at Livadia. Then, they moved to their villa on the Baltic Sea for a month or two. In June they usually took a cruise on the family yacht. In August, they went to their hunting lodge in Poland, in September back to the Black Sea, and in November to Tsarskoe Selo for the winter.

Servants and signs of extravagance were everywhere. To break the gloom of the Russian winter, the royal train often carried thousands of blooming flowers north to the imperial family from the Black Sea. To the delight of family members, Nicholas began ordering astronomically valuable Easter gifts, the famous imperial Easter eggs created by master craftsman Carl Fabergé. One fabulous egg was covered with gems and contained a tiny working model of the Trans-Siberian Railway.

Unlike his father, Nicholas did not enjoy the responsibilities of governing. Confrontations with strong-willed relatives and officials were not to his taste, and he hesitated to express his opinions directly, even to his government ministers. More than once, ministers left meetings feeling that the tsar had approved of their proposals or actions, only to find in a day or two a regretful note dismissing them from their posts.

As tsar, he was more a symbol of authority than a real leader who drew up policy ideas and carried them out. His chief concerns, besides his family, were to preserve the dynasty, to maintain the tsar's autocratic powers, and to strengthen the church. He had few plans beyond these traditional, conservative goals. Under Nicholas, government drifted

> *As a child, Nicholas ate the simplest foods, bathed in cold water, and even was obliged to go hungry on occasion. Heir of a dynasty that possessed vast lands, rich palaces, such priceless treasures as the Great Hermitage art collection and such royal gems as the 195-carat Orlov diamond and the 40-carat Polar Star ruby, he was obliged to sleep on an army cot, with a hard pallet for a mattress.*
> —W. BRUCE LINCOLN
> American historian

along like a huge rusty ship that was barely sea-worthy — its engines old and its hull leaking. The danger signs were there to see or — if the tsar wished —to ignore.

In 1898 Sergei Witte was the tsar's finance minister. A practical and insightful political operative, he had also been a businessman for many years. He was a statesman who clearly was in a position to perceive the country's ragged economic condition.

The belief had gained widespread acceptance that the impending 20th century would see new forms of government emphasizing social and economic

This ornate, jewel-encrusted creation is an example of Nicholas's spectacular extravagance. He ordered the clock and other priceless pieces from the French designer Carl Fabergé as Easter gifts for his family.

THE BETTMANN ARCHIVE

equality. Witte knew that, realistically, the 19th century was already at an end and that Russia was a chronically backward country, but he also knew that a revolutionary tide might come crashing against the gates at any time. Russia's peasant population had known the woes of poverty for generations. Only piecemeal reforms had been granted by Alexander III, and Nicholas tended to ignore the peasants' situation. Making matters worse, Nicholas felt extremely insecure in Witte's presence. In fact, when Witte asked for Nicholas's views on the emerging crisis, silence was the tsar's only answer.

Oblivious to rumblings beneath the surface, Nicholas was satisfied with reports officials handed him that charted steady progress for Russia's industries. What he had seen exhibited at the All-Russian Exposition of Trade and Industry at Nizhni-Novgorod soon after his coronation was sufficient proof to Nicholas that industrial and economic advances were being achieved.

Unemployed men pass the time at Moscow's Khitrov Market in the 1890s. Increasing industrialization was creating a class of workers who suffered its ill effects. At the same time famine wracked the peasantry for three years, beginning in 1891.

W.A.Rogers

3

The Russo-Japanese War

Under Nicholas's father, Russia had enjoyed a decade of peace. Alexander was wary of entangling military alliances and far-flung colonial ventures, preferring instead to unite his mammoth empire, and strengthen his own authority and that of the Orthodox church. Under Nicholas, the consolidation of the empire and conservative drive in government continued. For the most part, Nicholas lacked his father's realistic view of the European balance of power. Nevertheless, probably the most important diplomatic accomplishment of Nicholas's reign was the 1894 defensive alliance with France known as the Dual Alliance. In 1892, under Nicholas's father, an *Entente Cordiale* had been established with the French. The Dual Alliance was built upon this earlier diplomacy. It served as a check on German and Austrian ambitions in eastern Europe and the Balkans (the mountainous region in the southeastern European peninsula).

Nicholas, however, was uncommonly naive, and was ill-prepared to deal with the sly and ruthless

The Russians are defending the interests and supremacy of the white race against the increasing domination of the yellow race. Therefore, our sympathies must lie with Russia.
—WILHELM II
emperor of Germany

A cartoon summarizes the Russo-Japanese War of 1904–05. The United States, France, Britain, and Germany watch intently as Nicholas anxiously ponders his pieces and Japan coolly surveys the chessboard. The size of the antagonists suggests a David-and-Goliath parallel.

März-Stürme.

A 1905 German cartoon portrays Nicholas beset by "March storms" blown by the Japanese, a reference to their invasion of Russian-held Manchuria. The legend attributes Nicholas's problems to his attachment to antiquated ways.

statesmen who roamed the corridors of Europe's governments. There was probably no better example than his cousin Wilhelm II, the German *kaiser*, or emperor. Though roundly despised by the Russian imperial family and most of Europe's royalty for his arrogance, selfishness, bad manners, and posturing, Wilhelm could not be ignored. The Prussian military machine had rolled over much of northern Europe during the past 40 years, seizing "German" territories from weaker neighbors and creating a unified German empire under Hohenzollern kings of Prussia. By the 1890s Germany's industrial economy was booming, and it was well on the way to a world empire with important possessions in Africa and outposts in China. In short, Germany was already a major world industrial and military power, something that Nicholas could not claim for Russia.

Wilhelm II came to the German throne six years before Nicholas became tsar. He liked to act the older brother and tutor to his impressionable cousin. The German played on the Russian's weakness for military ceremonies, making Nicholas an honorary officer in the German army and losing no opportunity to stage impressive military or naval reviews in his honor. More important, he fostered a correspondence with Nicholas lasting from 1894 to 1904.

Nicholas called for an international disarmament conference in 1898 — one of his boldest moves ever. It was scheduled to be held at The Hague, capital of the Netherlands, from May to July 1899. Nicholas was very much interested in the possibilities for peace in Europe and elsewhere. He was also aware that arms cost money. His government was having trouble paying for new weapons and equipment. Yet not everyone was pleased with the tsar's idea. France began to worry that his conference would mean having to accept the boundaries set by the victorious Germans in the 1871 Franco-Prussian War. The French wanted eventually to regain all its lost territory, especially the area on its eastern border known as Alsace-Lorraine.

Nicholas meets his cousin Kaiser Wilhelm II of Germany prior to World War I, in which their countries went to war against each other. Nicholas was easily manipulated by Wilhelm, who maintained a decade-long correspondence with the tsar leading up to Russia's disastrous war with Japan, which Wilhelm encouraged for Germany's benefit.

To Wilhelm II, this disarmament conference was based upon a "mass of Russian hypocrisy, twaddle, and lies." When the conference was held, Germany's representatives did everything they could to destroy the purpose of the conference. Disarmament was never discussed. French fears and German arrogance made the project a failure.

In his cables, Wilhelm plied the tsar with his ideas and helpful suggestions, most of which were to his and Germany's advantage. At every turn, he encouraged Nicholas in his reactionary, anti-democratic beliefs, fueled his racial prejudice against Jews and East Asian peoples, encouraged Russian adventures in the Far East, and tried to build a personal alliance between the two monarchs. "Dear Nicky," Wilhelm would begin. How, he would ask, could Nicholas support an alliance with republican governments such as France when Germany and Russia had so much in common? "Dear Willy," Nicholas would reply. These issues, he would say, must be discussed further.

Acting entirely on the basis of personal diplomacy, Wilhelm pursued the idea of an alliance between Russia and Germany. In one of his meetings with Nicholas, the wily German just happened to have a treaty document in his pocket, and he soon convinced the tsar to sign it. Fortunately for Russia, both Nicholas's and Wilhelm's ministers exploded when they heard of it. Wilhelm's chancellor threatened to resign, and Nicholas's foreign minister convinced the tsar that the treaty was completely incompatible with the existing alliance with France. Rather than provoke a major realignment of powers in Europe on the basis of two cousins' impractical dreams, Nicholas and Wilhelm quietly scrapped the "Willy-Nicky" treaty. The episode revealed both Wilhelm's tendency to undertake major policy decisions without consulting his government and Nicholas's openness to flattery. In addition, it pointed to Nicholas's lifelong tendency to confuse personal relationships with matters of state.

Kaiser Wilhelm's efforts to interest Nicholas and Russia in the Far East were more successful. Wilhelm wanted the Russians to become bogged down on the Pacific coast so that Germany would have a freer hand in eastern Europe. In fact, Russia needed little encouragement because the tsars had been seeking a warm-water port on Russia's Pacific coast, which lies just far enough north to be blocked by ice for several months each winter. Russia coveted the Liaotung Peninsula in Manchuria and its excellent harbor at Port Arthur (or Lushun).

To acquire Port Arthur, Russia first had to evict the Japanese, which they did in 1895, and then force a long lease from the Chinese, who were too weak to resist the demands of any European power. By 1900 Russia had occupied the rest of Manchuria and built a railroad connecting the new Trans-Siberian Railway with the peninsula. Had Nicholas and his ministers stopped at that, all might have been well, but they did not. With the approval of the government, a group of Russian adventurers calling themselves the Yalu Timber Company moved into the Korean peninsula, which the Japanese regarded as their sphere of influence. The Japanese felt threatened and provoked.

Japan's growing military power in the Far East instigated Wilhelm II to sketch the idea on which this 1895 drawing was based. It is a dramatic illustration of Wilhelm's appeal to prejudice, to which Nicholas was all too susceptible.

Twice during the next four years, Japan sent top-level delegations to St. Petersburg to try to resolve the dispute, and twice the diplomats were insulted, abused, and sent home without ever seeing the tsar, who had nothing but contempt for the "little yellow, tailless monkeys." Through it all, the German kaiser's letters, signed as usual, "Willy," urged "Nicky" to stand up for Russia's rights and fight the "yellow peril." Then, too, more than a few of Nicholas's ministers thought that a "small, victorious war" might be a useful distraction from mounting peasant rebellions and other domestic problems. Nicholas disliked his country being on the brink of war; the uncertainty was almost more than he could bear.

Clamoring to join battle with the Japanese, the Russians felt assured of their military — as well as

Despite its great size, Russia had no ports with unrestricted access to the sea that were not blocked by ice in the winter, and so coveted Port Arthur. To secure this outlet to the Pacific, Russia evicted the Japanese from Manchuria in 1895 and forced concessions from the much weaker Chinese.

THE RUSSIAN EMPIRE AT THE TIME OF THE REVOLUTION

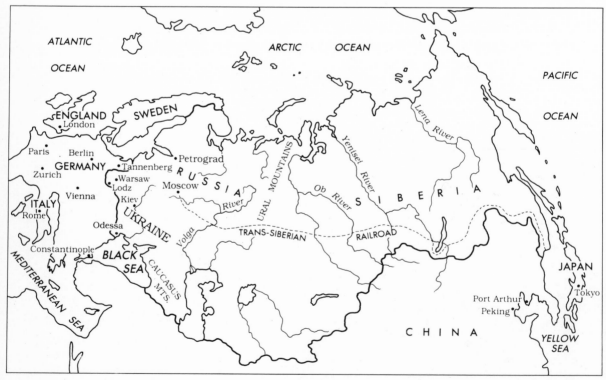

cultural — superiority. They would soon meet with an unpleasant surprise. At midnight on February 6, 1904, a Japanese fleet sailed unnoticed into the unprotected outer harbor of Port Arthur, sank two Russian battleships and a cruiser, and blockaded the port. Stunned, Nicholas wrote bitterly in his diary, "This without a declaration of war. May God come to our aid." But Japan was prepared and Russia was not. At the moment of attack, Japan had 150,000 troops ready for combat, substantially more than the combined forces of regular Russian troops, railway guards, and garrison soldiers in the Far East. Under Admiral Yevgeny Alexeev, the Russian navy was advised against an aggressive battle, which played into the hands of the Japanese. Having gone on the offensive at sea and successfully blockaded much of Russia's Far Eastern fleet, Japan sent masses of troops through the Korean peninsula, into Manchuria, and toward the Liaotung Peninsula and Port Arthur. While the war had begun at Port Arthur, it would reach a dismal conclusion for the Russians with the defeat at Mukden.

During the next few months nothing but disastrous news reached the tsar. In April the heroic Admiral Stepan Makarov and 700 of his crewmen perished while steaming back into Port Arthur in the battleship *Petropavlovsk* when the vessel struck mines set by the Japanese that Makarov had miraculously not triggered when his ships had left the harbor.

As the Japanese land forces came ashore, the Russian cruiser *Variag* did nothing to stop them. The

Russian warships ply the harbor at Port Arthur in 1904. In an attack there in April, the Japanese sank the *Variag* (second from right) and disabled the *Peresvyet* (at right).

News of the outbreak of the war stunned and stirred Russia. Scarcely anyone had expected it, since the vast majority of Russians had only the vaguest interest in Manchuria. Nevertheless, the reaction was universal: Russia had been attacked.
—SERGEI S. OLDENBURG
Russian historian

Japanese then successfully attacked the cruiser. It had been the Russians' hope that their defensive strategy would wear down the Japanese invaders. Remaining constantly on the offensive, the Japanese were bound to lose ships and men. However, the Russian fleet was handicapped without Admiral Makarov. Although the Japanese subsequently lost two battleships — the *Hatsuse* and the *Yashima* — they still had the brilliant leadership of Admiral Heihachiro Togo.

General Alexei Kuropatkin was the commander of the Russian infantry at the Battle of the Yalu River. (The Yalu flows toward the Bay of Korea and forms part of the border between North Korea and China.) Kuropatkin believed in remaining on the defensive until enough troops were available for a major counterattack against the Japanese invaders. "No battle before we are in superior force," he said. Here again the Japanese launched an offensive. The Russians had thought they would stand and fight, inflict as much damage as possible on the Japanese, then retreat. Japanese forces outnumbered the Russians by four to one. Although the Russians held to their plan, their retreat allowed the Japanese to take the high ground. On May 1, 1904, Nicholas's army lost their first encounter on land against Japan.

On May 26 the Russians were driven from their fortifications on a hill at Nanshan, Manchuria. Roughly half of the Russian unit was destroyed. As Kuropatkin slowly gathered his forces, orders were given for a more aggressive policy. On June 14, 35,000 Japanese troops met 25,000 Russian troops who had dug in at Telissu. After losing almost one-fifth of their unit in casualties, the Russians were sent running in disarray. The situation was no better at sea for Nicholas's empire. After Makarov's successor was killed in battle, a nobleman named Prince Ukhtomsky took charge of the Russian fleet in August, but Admiral Togo once again emerged successful. Russia was now helpless to prevent the complete blockade of Port Arthur.

Nicholas's war against the Japanese was coming to a standstill. After a fierce stand-off at the Battle of Shaho in October 1904, and an earlier Russian defeat at nearby Liao-yang, the Russians fought desperately at Mukden (modern Shenyang in northeastern China). Kuropatkin's armies countered the Japanese and managed to escape without being encircled. The Russians, however, had lost 97,000 troops while the Japanese casualties amounted to about half this number.

In St. Petersburg, the government faced difficult problems. First, Nicholas had to be dissuaded by his family from recklessly placing himself in personal command of his Far Eastern troops. The government everywhere faced military incompetence and lack of planning. Russian land forces were connected with their main supply depots only by the Trans-Siberian Railway, which stretched out over thousands of miles and was useless in winter and early spring. The major portion of the imperial navy was in the Baltic Sea, not in the Pacific, so it would have to be moved to be useful. The chief of the Russian admiralty was known to be drawn to "fast

Members of a Russian scouting party are guarded by their captors, a unit of the Japanese Second Division.

Japanese Admiral Heihachiro Togo wore the symbols of his rank into his ninth decade. Under Togo's command, the Japanese navy decimated the antiquated Russian fleet.

women and slow ships." Moving the fleet would require months of planning and travel. The Japanese, on the other hand, had no such problems and from the outset maintained an overwhelming advantage in the war.

Facing complete humiliation — he would be the first Russian tsar to lose a war to an Asian nation — Nicholas gambled on the ability of his imperial navy. With the constant encouragement of Wilhelm II, he ordered the Russian Baltic Fleet under Admiral Zinovi Rozhdestvensky to begin the long voyage to the Far East. From disastrous beginning to devastating end, the great voyage was a lesson in how not to run a navy.

In October, barely out of the Baltic Sea, the admiral encountered a group of boats that he thought looked suspicious. He feared they were Japanese gunboats in disguise, 12,000 miles from home.

After blowing several from the water with his heavy guns, the admiral discovered them to be English fishing trawlers. Embarrassed and unwilling to delay the fleet any longer, Rozhdestvensky ignored the survivors and steamed on. The so-called "Dogger Bank Incident" caused an uproar in Europe, brought England to the verge of war with Russia, and ended only with payment of damages assessed by the International Court of Justice, which, ironically, Nicholas had helped to establish.

For seven months, the world (including Japan) followed the progress of the regrouped Russian fleet. On the afternoon of May 27, 1905, the Russian fleet, led by eight battleships in neat double rows, entered the Tsushima Straits between Japan and Korea, where Admiral Togo and the Japanese waited. Togo, spreading his ships along a two-mile line, blocked the oncoming column of ships by turning his own ships sideways and perpendicular to the approaching squadron. Thus Togo's ships could turn most of their guns toward the Russians and fire simultaneously. Forty-five minutes of shelling destroyed or disabled most of the Russian vessels. The remainder were attacked by torpedo boats. By the following day, when the action was over, the Japanese

> *I beg you to be patient and, with full realization of Russia's strength, patiently to await further developments. Our initial steps entail the movement of troops through vast spaces. . . . Patience, patience, and patience, gentlemen.*
> —ALEXEI KUROPATKIN
> Russian general

In the climactic battle of the war in May 1905, Russia's Baltic fleet sags under heavy bombardment by Japanese ships in the Tsushima Straits, separating Japan and Korea. Japan's success sealed its status as a major power.

AP/WIDE WORLD

had sunk or captured most of the Russian fleet. Japan lost only three torpedo boats.

The news of the greatest naval engagement in a century devastated Nicholas, who received it aboard the imperial train. It also sent shock waves around the world, for it required European powers to take account of the new world power — Japan — and to revise their methods of naval warfare.

Almost six months before Tsushima, the Russians had lost Port Arthur. The Japanese had shelled it with heavy guns, stormed the heights, and forced its surrender in January 1905. This battle cost 58,000 Japanese lives, while the Russians lost some 25,000 troops.

Having lost the war on the battlefield, Russia proceeded to win part of it at the conference table. Nicholas recalled to duty one of the ablest men in Russian government, Sergei Witte, whom Nicholas had hired and fired several times in the past. Always the realist, Witte drily observed, "When a sewer has to be cleaned, they send for Witte." His task was to represent Russia at the peace conference in Ports-

During their blockade of the harbor at Port Arthur in 1904, Japanese ships undertake a night bombardment of the Russian fleet and shore fortifications.

Theodore Roosevelt tends to his papers in 1914. In 1905, during his second term as president of the United States, he mediated an end to the Russo-Japanese War, an achievement for which he won the Nobel Peace Prize the following year.

mouth, New Hampshire, mediated by United States President Theodore Roosevelt.

Witte launched a very successful public relations campaign to win over the journalists and American public. In doing so, he made it difficult for the aloof Japanese diplomats to present their demands effectively. Japan, in financial trouble because of the war, had to accept a compromise that left Russia still in possession of much Pacific territory. Nevertheless, Japan was able to secure part of its influence in Korea. The Russians were required to withdraw their forces from Kwantung, (the southern part of Liaotung Peninsula), much of Manchuria, and the southern half of Sakhalin Island. Port Arthur, of course, had to be given up as well. Theo-

Sergei Witte, finance minister from 1892 to 1903 under both Alexander III and Nicholas, was named by Nicholas to represent Russia in the peace negotiations at Portsmouth, New Hampshire, in 1905. He adroitly saved for Russia some of what it had lost in battle, preserving its control over part of Manchuria.

The tsar is not free. He talks now to one, now to another. He listens to his uncles, his mother, Pobedonostsev. He is a pitiful, insignificant, even an unkind person.

—LEO TOLSTOY
Russian writer

dore Roosevelt received a Nobel Peace Prize for his diplomatic efforts.

For Russia, the importance of the war was that it revealed a government riddled with incompetence, a once grand navy reduced to scrap metal, and an army saddled with haughty generals who could not win a single major battle. In a flash, the veils were lifted to expose a government unable to protect vital national interests and increasingly unable to govern at all. At the head of the government, attending the memorial services and visiting the disabled, just as they had done after the tragedy at Khodynka Field, were the tsar and tsarina. Nicholas, however, still clung to his often unspoken conviction that Russia needed no more reforms.

Two years before the war, Nicholas had received a letter from Count Leo Tolstoy, the author of the novels *War and Peace* and *Anna Karenina*. In it the famed Russian writer tried to make the tsar aware of the disaster that awaited his people and his rule unless he righted certain injustices. Nicholas's people were suffering the consequences of a backwardness too long left unremedied.

The tsar's advisers, Tolstoy wrote, were weak men who could be molded and made to obey. What they lacked were exactly the qualities needed to assist a ruler in times of crisis: daring and imagination. Tolstoy urged the tsar to understand that autocratic rule would not suffice for much longer. The Russian people were beginning to chafe under increasingly harsh treatment. Tolstoy warned that revolution would prove unavoidable if the tsar continued to insulate himself from the people's wishes and refused to redistribute the land then monopolized by rich gentry.

Leo Tolstoy was one of the premier Russian writers of the second half of the 19th century. Though born into a noble family, he became a severe critic of the imperial Russian state. Prior to the war with Japan, he wrote a prescient letter to Nicholas, warning him of impending revolution if he did not liberalize his regime.

4

Bloody Sunday and the Revolution of 1905

In the early hours of January 22, 1905, a worker named Ivan Vasilev penned a note to his wife and young son as he prepared to join a workers' march on the Winter Palace to present a petition to his tsar. "If I am killed," he wrote, "then do not weep. Raise Vaniura [Ivan] and tell him that I died a martyr for the freedom and happiness of the people." And while Vasilev and others like him made their preparations, the governor of St. Petersburg made his. Some 12,000 soldiers and cavalrymen were brought into the city, giving St. Petersburg the air of a battle waiting to happen. As the soldiers were given ammunition, they were told — falsely — that the workers intended to seize and destroy the Winter Palace and murder the tsar, his family, and government leaders.

At dawn workers began gathering at different staging points before beginning the march to the Winter Palace. Their leader, Father Gapon, a 34-year-old priest and part-time police informant from the Ukraine, had apparently given up his police work and devoted himself to the workers' causes.

Things are bad in the interior. Agrarian disorders are starting. They are burning factories and plundering. The ministries fidget, the tsar fidgets, the police fidget. They all talk about the oncoming slaughter.
—ALEXEI A. BOBRINSKY
Russian count, diary entry
from January 1905

A priest named Georgy Gapon leads a huge contingent of workers on January 22, 1905, to petition the tsar for an eight-hour day, a minimum daily wage of one ruble (50 cents), and representative government. The day became known as Bloody Sunday after soldiers fired on the unarmed throng, touching off a growing revolt.

The growing number of workers in industry was augmented by the men employed in expansion of the railway network. Included in the project was the construction of the Trans-Siberian railway, which was begun under Alexander III in 1891 and completed during the Russo-Japanese War.

He wanted, in particular, to lead a grand march and meet with the tsar. In the weeks preceding the march, Gapon seized on a strike at the Putilov steel works as the call to action and began delivering rousing speeches in favor of a petition to the "Little Father" asking his protection and justice for the workers of St. Petersburg and their families. "Supposing the tsar will not receive us and will not read our petition?" he shouted to crowds. "Then we have no tsar!" they shouted back.

On the morning of January 22, 30,000 men, women, and children began moving down the broad avenues that converged on the Winter Palace. Carefully instructed by Gapon and dressed in their Sunday best, they carried religious icons and portraits of the tsar and tsarina — not weapons. On each avenue, the tsar's soldiers had erected barricades to prevent the mob from attacking the palace. As the

workers pressed on, soldiers were ordered to fire, and they did. Bullets crashed into icons, portraits, barriers, and bodies, turning the orderly march into a hellish scramble for safety. The worst slaughter occurred in the square directly opposite the Winter Palace itself. Bloody Sunday, as it came to be called, took the lives of between 90 and 200 workers and as many as 800 were wounded. Among the fallen was Ivan Vasilev. Father Gapon escaped the scene but was soon denounced as an informer. His body was found hanged a year later in Finland.

Why did Bloody Sunday happen, and why in 1905? It probably would not have happened without the rapid growth of a reform-minded professional class and a new industrial working class. The latter was the product of Alexander III and Nicholas's intense efforts to develop Russian industry and build a major railroad network. With these industrial workers came strikes for better wages and conditions. At the time of the Putilov strike, no worker was paid enough to support a family. In order for a family to live and eat, mothers and children had to work, too. There were severe housing shortages, so severe in some areas that workers labored and slept in shifts, one bed serving three or more people.

When Nicholas came to the throne, strikes were a rarity. By 1905 Russia was experiencing strikes at a rate of 500 each year. Reformers, including doctors, educators, and writers, tried to publicize the social abuses and force change from within. Stirring the kettle of discontent were radicals and subversives who wished to overthrow the tsarist regime and start over. Coming on the heels of military disaster and a long period of social agitation, the workers' strike at the Putilov factory was the spark that led to Bloody Sunday.

As this tragedy unfolded, Nicholas was 20 miles from the Winter Palace, which he rarely visited. For weeks, his ministers had ignored or minimized the importance of the march. Only the day before it occurred did they at last mention it to the tsar. By then, they were so thoroughly alarmed at the potential for mob violence that they and Nicholas decided it was out of the question for even a rep-

Father Gapon, the catalyst for the 1905 revolution, played no effective role after Bloody Sunday. From his exile in Finland he wrote Nicholas to tell of the irretrievable loss to the tsar of his subjects' allegiance and to pronounce a terrible curse: "Moral connection between thee and them may never more be. . . . Let all the blood that has to be shed, hangman, fall upon thee and thy kindred!"

resentative of the tsar to be seen accepting "demands" from the rabble. So, as several hundred of his royal subjects were being shot to death in the heart of the capital, Nicholas was safely at home with his family at Tsarskoe Selo.

Had Nicholas heard the workers out and addressed some of their problems, the course of Russian history might have been very different. A gentle, generous man at heart, Nicholas had an excellent reputation for receiving and granting petitions from individual subjects, as long as they were presented man-to-man. He would not, however, listen to or deal with a mob.

What followed was a decade of rapid upheaval and change in which Nicholas, instead of steering the ship of state, was usually dragging its anchor.

The upheavals did not end on Bloody Sunday; they were just beginning. In February, a few weeks later, a revolutionary tossed a bomb into Grand Duke Sergei Alexandrovich's lap as his carriage was leaving the Kremlin, the traditional seat of government in Moscow. The attack had come from the "Combat Detachment" of the Social Revolutionary party (SR), led by Victor Chernov. The group demanded an immediate end to the tsar's autocracy. The blast violently ended the grand duke's life.

In the face of continuing strikes, peasant uprisings, and military mutinies (the most famous of which was aboard the battleship *Potemkin*), Nicholas proposed too little too late. He proclaimed religious tolerance in an effort to halt pogroms against Jews, and he repealed a few punitive laws aimed at minorities. He also proposed the creation of a representative assembly, though one with only "consultative" powers.

Nothing worked, and by October the entire country was in the grip of a massive general strike, called by some the most complete and effective general strike in history. The first to strike were the railroad workers on the Moscow-Kazan line on October 7. Workers throughout the rail system followed their example. During the ensuing panic, Pobedonostsev was forced to leave office. By October 17 the entire rail system lay dead, and in St. Petersburg and other major cities virtually all business and work ceased. Even the tsar's Imperial Ballet joined the strike. Workers led by the Marxist revolutionary organizer Leon Trotsky formed a workers' *soviet*, or council, to act as a provisional government in St. Petersburg. Trotsky was to become a leading figure in the revolution that would take place in November of 1917 — the Bolshevik Revolution. Trotsky's soviet attempted to function as the actual government, ignoring the tsar.

The Bolsheviks had their origin in a conference of the Social Democratic party, held in London, England, in 1903. This party was one of the most radical organizations in Russia at the time. When a faction led by the young revolutionary Vladimir Lenin gained the most votes, the term *bolshevik* —

The defeat in the war with Japan helped lead to rioting in the army in 1905. Disorder spread to the navy; at Odessa in June there occurred a mutiny on the battleship *Potemkin*, shown here. The ship roamed the Black Sea for a few days before putting in at a Romanian port, where the rebellious sailors were taken into custody.

from the Russian for "majority" — stuck as their name. Through this party Lenin intended to overthrow the tsar's autocratic rule and put into practice the economic and political ideas of the 19th-century German social philosopher Karl Marx. Marx argued in his writings that capitalist societies are part of a necessary but temporary stage in social development. He believed that the working class (or "proletariat") would overthrow the capitalist system and that capitalism would inevitably give way to socialism, the rule of the working class. Lenin was certain, however, that only violent revolution could bring down the tsar and, ultimately, capitalism.

Russia had its own important revolutionary thinkers. One of these was Georgy Plekhanov, who founded the Russian Marxist movement. As leader-in-exile of the Social Democratic party from the 1880s until the early 1900s, Plekhanov greatly influenced the young Lenin. As the Bolsheviks gained power within this movement, Lenin and Plekhanov co-founded the journal *Iskra* (*The Spark*). Although frequently in agreement with the Bolsheviks over the years, Plekhanov could not side with them completely. Finally, he broke with them and remained an opponent until his death in May 1918.

Another figure who contributed to 19th-century Russian political theory was Prince Peter Kropotkin. Not a follower of Marx's ideas, Kropotkin wrote *Mutual Aid*, a book that discusses the possibilities for peaceful cooperation and for societies without government. Thus he helped create the political idea of anarchism — arguing that the best society would flourish if governments were abolished.

Russian literary figures were also caught up in the political tensions of the period. Maxim Gorky (the pen name of Alexei Peshkov; the name Gorky was derived from the Russian for "bitter") was one of the most prominent of these. From a working class family and forced to support himself as a child, Gorky knew the plight of Russia's peasants and factory workers firsthand. By 1899 Gorky had become involved with the Social Democratic party, and he would eventually participate in the revolution of 1905. Although intensely critical of Lenin's repres-

In October 1905 Leon Trotsky helped form the St. Petersburg Soviet of Workers' Deputies. The man who would play a vital role in Nicholas's downfall 12 years later passed a sweeping judgment on the tsar: "This 'charmer,' without will, without aim, without imagination, was more awful than all the tyrants of ancient and modern history."

sive measures that stamped out opposition to the Bolshevik revolution, Gorky gave Lenin his support once the revolution was victorious. In Gorky's autobiographical stories and novels one encounters the essence of the Russian revolutionary period.

During the political crisis of 1905, Nicholas was surrounded by bewildered, petrified ministers, all of his own choosing, and by generals who were only too willing to shoot civilians. Nicholas received good advice, not from the ministers or generals, but from his mother, the Dowager Empress Maria, who said, "Call Witte." When Count Witte — the title was his reward for his work at the negotiations with the Japanese at Portsmouth, New Hampshire — arrived, he made it plain that Nicholas had only two choices: a military dictatorship or creation of a constitution, a legislature, and some previously nonexistent civil liberties, such as freedom of speech and press. Predictably, Nicholas opted first for military dictatorship, but he could find no one suitable for the role. Grand Duke Nikolai refused the "honor" by threatening to kill himself in the tsar's presence if he persisted. The grand duke forcefully suggested that Nicholas choose Witte's second option. Thus Nicholas reluctantly gave consent for the creation of a constitutional monarchy. "There was no way out but to make the sign of the cross and do what the world demanded," the tsar wrote Alexandra.

On October 30, with Nicholas's nervous approval, Witte issued the October Manifesto, in which the tsar guaranteed civil rights, agreed to call a *duma* (legislature) elected by the people, and stated that thereafter all laws must be approved by the legislature. In other words, Nicholas gave up his right to make laws on his own authority. The manifesto claimed that "no law shall come into force without the consent of the State Duma." Witte's bold manifesto was viewed with horror in conservative circles and with dismay and disappointment by revolutionaries. Trotsky, perhaps the most outspoken of them at this time, voiced dissatisfaction: "A constitution is given, but the autocracy remains. . . . The proletariat wants neither the police hooligan . . . nor the liberal broker Witte. . . ." Their unity

AP/WIDE WORLD

Vladimir Lenin led the radical faction of the Russian Social Democratic party from exile for almost two decades until he returned to Russia in 1917 to take control of the revolution. His group, called the Bolsheviks, favored a closed party membership distinguished by control from the top.

The fourth Russian Duma, or parliament, sits in Petrograd (formerly St. Petersburg) on March 16, 1917. The revolution of 1905 forced Nicholas to agree in October of that year to the establishment of such a representative assembly. Elections were held the following spring, and the first session opened in May.

broken, the revolutionaries began squabbling among themselves. By December, Witte was able to overpower and capture most of the members of the St. Petersburg soviet. Elsewhere, the tsar's troops ruthlessly put down uprisings in Moscow and the countryside.

Neither Witte nor Nicholas was enthusiastic about a constitutional government, Witte because he had become more favorable to military solutions in the first two difficult months, and Nicholas because he had been forced into it. As time passed and the promise of October had to be translated into the actions of the spring of 1906, the tsar's concept of constitutional monarchy underwent a crucial change. In April the tsar and his ministers met to discuss changes in the legal codes called the "Fundamental Laws." "The question still torments me," Nicholas said to his ministers, "do I have the right to change the form of that authority which my ancestors bequeathed to me? I was fully aware of what I was doing when I issued the Manifest of October 17th [October 30] and I am resolved to see it through to the end. But I am not convinced that

UPI/BETTMANN NEWSPHOTOS

62

this requires me to renounce the right of supreme power and change the definition of it that has existed for 109 years. . . ."

His ministers quickly pointed out that this amounted to a denial of constitutional monarchy and urged him to choose his words carefully. Article One of the earlier Fundamental Laws had stated that the tsar's power was "autocratic and unlimited." His ministers wanted him to do away with the term "unlimited." Count Witte told the tsar that "the entire future of Russia" depended on whether he chose to keep "unlimited" power. The new Article Four, suggested by his ministers, would say that the tsar's power was "supreme and autocratic." Now Nicholas's ministers turned anxiously to the tsar to hear his decision. "I have decided to retain the wording of the Council of Ministers," Nicholas said. "The Autocrat of All the Russias" had agreed at last to limit his power.

In fact, Nicholas and Alexandra never understood the fundamental change in his role after October 30, and they frequently crossed the line separating constitutionality and autocracy. Worse still, the tsar soon tired of Witte and replaced him with a doddering nonentity, Ivan Goremykin. Aside from being probably too old for this position, Goremykin lacked any qualifications for serving as prime minister and chairman of the council of ministers.

The shape of the new order was set by a new election law for the Duma and by the tsar's Fundamental Laws. The election law gave virtually every man the vote. The Fundamental Laws stated what the Duma could and could not do and added a few surprises. About 40 percent of the entire government budget was to be exempt from Duma approval, and whole areas, such as foreign policy, were reserved for the exclusive attention of Nicholas and his ministers. The "Laws" also turned the tsar's very conservative Council of Advisers into an upper house of the legislature. The tsar retained veto power — the right to reject any piece of legislation that the body drafted.

When the first elections were held, the tsar and his ministers were shocked. Instead of voting for

THE BETTMANN ARCHIVE

Karl Marx sits for his portrait in London. His theories of class struggle and the ultimate overthrow of capitalism inspired Lenin and the Social Democrats. When the Bolsheviks began governing Russia in 1917, Lenin left his own stamp on Marx's ideas in his role as the first leader to put them to practical use.

the tsar and his conservative candidates, Nicholas's beloved peasants voted overwhelmingly for candidates ranging politically from moderate to radical. The resulting legislature was soon at odds with Nicholas and the ministers. It was dissolved by the tsar after only 73 days. In protest, 200 members, ranging from moderate to radical viewpoints, met in Vyborg, Finland, and called on the people to pay no taxes until a new Duma was seated. Nicholas jailed them all, and declared them ineligible for election to the new Duma.

Despite intensive efforts by the tsar's officials, the elections for the Second Duma (there was to be a third and a fourth) produced results similar to the first, and the government and Duma were soon deadlocked. Again, the tsar dissolved the assembly. But before calling new elections, Nicholas and his bright, able replacement for Goremykin, Peter Stolypin, decided to change the rules by altering the electoral law. In defense of this irregular act, Nicholas stated that it was his right to cancel what he had granted, and that he would answer only to God, from whom he derived his authority. The new law cut peasant and worker representation and increased upper-class representation. Only in that way did Nicholas succeed in creating a legislature that he and Stolypin could work with. But Nicholas's action revealed how fragile was his commitment to constitutional government.

The Duma encompassed the wide spectrum of political groups that carried on their struggle over what would soon be the corpse of tsarist Russia. Although the representation changed each time a new Duma was elected, the parties ranged from the extreme conservatives and nationalists to the Constitutional Democratic party (the Kadets, as they were called), consisting of zemstvo, or local government, representatives and various reformers. More radical than the Kadets, the Social Democratic party held 65 seats in the Second Duma. In addition to these were the more moderate parties, the Progressives and the Octobrists, or Conservatives.

Prime Minister Stolypin, perhaps the most effective administrator in Nicholas's Russia and maybe in all Europe, set out to attack the country's two biggest problems. Nicholas was fond of pointing out that he and the statesman had the same birthday, which happened to fall on the feast day of Job the Sufferer. Job, whose story of misfortune and faith is told at length in the Bible, was sometimes compared to the beleaguered tsar.

Stolypin's policy was twofold. First, he cracked down on the mounting domestic violence by authorizing summary courts-martial to dispense instant justice. Stolypin himself once remarked: "Order first, reform later." The hangman's noose was used so widely against discontented villagers that it became known as "Stolypin's necktie." Vil-

Standing next to symbols of his authority — his throne, robe, and crown — Nicholas formally opens a session of the Duma. He retained many rights, including veto power over any act of the Duma, and he dissolved the first two Dumas until he got one that was more to his liking in November 1907.

A 1905 issue of a German magazine carries the headline
"Reception of the Zemstvo Delegation by the Tsar." Local governing bodies originally set up under Alexander
II, zemstvos provided much of the leadership in the 1905
revolution. Nicholas had only contempt for them and all
representative government.

lages were frequently raided to counteract unrest in Russia's peasants. Second, with Nicholas firmly in tow, Stolypin embarked on a program of economic and social legislation so far-reaching as to cause revolutionaries, such as Lenin, to become alarmed. They feared that if the tsar's government addressed and solved many of the people's grievances, then the reasons for overthrowing the tsar would disappear. The people might no longer listen to the radicals' calls for revolt and for a new government. Indeed, in 1905 there had been as many as 100,000 people involved in revolutionary groups; by 1911, only one-tenth that number were still active in trying to overthrow the government. By 1906 Lenin was forced to flee to Finland. Trotsky was exiled to Siberia but escaped to Vienna.

Stolypin's most ambitious program was agrarian reform, meaning a consolidation and redistribution of farm lands held in common by villages. Stolypin's famous "wager on the strong and sober" was designed to create a new type of peasant — the independent, landowning farmer. It worked well as far as it went — farm production did improve noticeably — but the nobility refused to follow Nicholas's example of selling off large tracts of land to the peasants. In fact, the basic farm legislation was rejected by the conservative upper house and had to be declared an "emergency" law by the tsar, as was his right, during a convenient recess of the Duma. In so doing, Nicholas overrode the outraged objections of his mother and most of the large imperial family. Stolypin's progressive programs greatly shocked many conservatives, and there is good reason to think that Dmitri Bogrov, the man who assassinated Stolypin during an opera performance in the city of Kiev on September 1, 1911, was in league with the prime minister's political foes.

Stolypin's assassination took place at a performance of the opera *Tale of Tsar Saltan* (1900) by Nikolai Rimsky-Korsakov, an important composer of the period and one who lived to see both the Russo-Japanese War and the 1905 Revolution. Stolypin was shot as he stood in the first row of the orchestra below the tsar's box in a theater filled with

A dancer appears in 1913 as the chief eunuch in the ballet set to the music of Nikolai Rimsky-Korsakov's *Scheherezade*. One of the leading Russian composers of the late 19th century, Rimsky-Korsakov took inspiration from the Asiatic influence on Russian history.

A painting by A. Rylov depicts Lenin fleeing arrest in
Russia in early 1906 by
crossing the frozen Gulf of
Finland, guided by two
Finns. He had returned to
Russia in December and instigated street fighting in
Moscow. But by then revo-
lutionary fervor among the
populace had dimmed under
the twin pressures of government reprisals and limited
reforms.

the tsar's own security police. The assassin was captured and whisked to an early execution before the
imperial authorities could complete a thorough
investigation.

Despite Stolypin's surprising new policies and the
radicals' fears, the threat of revolution was far from
over. A spark had been struck in 1905 that slowly
burned for another 12 years.

Nicholas hired and fired several unimpressive figures to fill the position of his prime minister, but
his choices were mediocre at best. These men had
been selected on the basis of their stubborn and
cautious resistance to new ideas. As Europe stood
on the brink of a world war, Nicholas installed as

Peter Stolypin, appointed Nicholas's prime minister in 1906, had this portrait taken in New York. He was one of the strongest officials to serve the tsar and succeeded both in calming the country and gaining Nicholas's assent to liberal measures. His policies made him enemies across the political spectrum, leading to his assassination in 1911.

the head of government an old man who, according to one ambassador, spent a great deal of time lounging on sofas and reading French novels.

Speaking to the departing prime minister, the perceptive Dowager Empress Maria delivered a devastating evaluation of the situation: "I see we are nearing some catastrophe and the tsar listens to no one but flatterers, not perceiving or even suspecting what goes on all around him. Why do you not decide to tell the tsar all you think and know . . . if it is not already too late?" The minister replied, correctly, that no one would listen to him or believe him, mainly because the tsarina thought him her enemy. In truth, Alexandra's rising influence over Nicholas, the man she called "Russia's Savior," and her efforts to purge all bearers of unwelcome news and criticism were to have fateful consequences for Russia and the imperial family.

5

The Great European War

In the summer of 1914 three emperors brought Europe to war and caused the eventual destruction of their dynasties and the empires they ruled. The three were Wilhelm II of Germany, Franz Josef of Austria-Hungary, and Nicholas of Russia. Unlike the mainly ceremonial king of England, each of the three possessed considerable influence over foreign affairs, the military, and internal governmental policies. Moreover, each monarch was directly responsible for committing his country to war.

Of the three, Franz Josef was the oldest and wisest. At age 84, he had ruled for 66 years and presided over a long and tumultuous period in the history of the Hapsburg empire. As emperor of Austria and king of Hungary, he was the glue that held together 50 million people of competing nationalities and languages. He, like Nicholas, faced a growing problem among the Slavic peoples of the Balkan peninsula, some of whom lived within the borders of his empire and wanted to establish their own governments. There was, in addition, a powerful movement called Pan-Slavism, spanning both empires,

Let Papa not plan war because war will mean the end of Russia and yourselves and you will lose to the last man.
—GREGORY RASPUTIN
Russian mystic, message to Nicholas warning him about joining World War I

Nicholas (left) is shown with another cousin who, in 1910, became head of a European royal house: George V of England. Their countries would fight as allies in World War I against Germany, Austria, and Turkey.

Having failed the previous year in their attempt to march into the heart of Germany, the Russians array howitzers in a defensive position outside Warsaw on June 30, 1915. By now the artillerymen were severely hindered by their lack of ammunition.

that had as its goal the unification of the Slavs into independent nations. It was Franz Josef's personal restraint that had prevented a Balkan crisis from erupting into a general European war only a few years earlier.

Wilhelm was the product of a highly military upbringing. He regarded himself as a peerless expert in military strategy and diplomat. The empire he ruled had been built on "blood and iron" by the brilliant German statesman Otto von Bismarck, whom Wilhelm had dismissed two years after coming to the throne in 1888. Bismarck's successors were less able than "the Iron Chancellor," and could not restrain Wilhelm from undertaking potentially disastrous diplomatic and military initiatives. His armies were the best trained, best equipped, and most experienced in Europe.

Wilhelm disregarded Bismarck's policy of maintaining friendly relations with Russia. Unlike Wilhelm I before him (whose funeral Nicholas had attended in 1888), the young kaiser refused to be Bismarck's pawn. He defied Bismarck's demands to uphold the "Reinsurance" treaty, which aimed to maintain peace between Austria-Hungary and Russia. Against the aging chancellor's advice, Wilhelm made it understood that Germany was committed to fight for Austria-Hungary if Emperor Franz Josef mobilized his troops against any enemy. Since Bismarck had strived to prevent conflict between Russia and Austria-Hungary, Wilhelm's break with previous German policy angered the Russians. Wilhelm pushed also for greater German economic involvement in the Near East (the area later known as the Middle East).

After diplomatic ties between France and Russia were mended and the two nations concluded the Dual Alliance (a military alliance), Germany and Russia became potential foes. The alliance meant that France and Russia would fight alongside each other in the event of war. Indeed, this alliance held until 1917, nearly the end of World War I.

Wilhelm had further provoked Russia in 1898 by paying a visit to Constantinople (Istanbul) in Turkey. This region was considered the "back door" to Russia. It also had long been a Russian ambition to control the nearby Bosporus, the strait that links the Black Sea and the Sea of Marmara. But in 1899 the Germans planned to build a railroad connecting the two seas. Such behavior was regarded with suspicion by the Russians, and Nicholas was gradually won over to seeing the advantages of opening an alliance with Great Britain during this period. Russia was outraged further in 1913 when a German general became commander not only of the Turkish detachment in Constantinople, but of the entire Turkish army.

Nicholas, though fascinated by military ceremony and tradition, was deeply fearful of war. He was one of the creators of the International Court of Justice in The Hague, the purpose of which was to resolve disputes before they reached the point of war. His key advisers were undistinguished, particularly the highly excitable Sergei Sazonov, his foreign minister. Like Franz Josef, Nicholas faced strong Slavic nationalist movements within his empire, and those movements enjoyed much public support. His

THE BETTMANN ARCHIVE

Otto von Bismarck, one of the premier European statesmen of the 19th century, helped forge the modern German nation. He was dismissed as chancellor in 1890 by Wilhelm II for his opposition to the kaiser's plans for social reform and for his intrigues against him in the Reichstag, or parliament.

Nicholas and his son, Alexis, stand before their army officers during World War I. Though a decade had passed, the army was still suffering from its defeat in the Russo-Japanese War.

army was theoretically the biggest in Europe, but was riddled with corruption and incompetence. Ten years after the disasters of the Russo-Japanese War, the Russian army was still in a deplorable state. It was the least battle-ready of all the three imperial armies.

The three empires were part of a complex system of alliances that formed a balance of power in Europe. For more than a decade the system had worked to preserve the peace by threatening to turn any conflicts between major powers into a general war. An attack on one country automatically brought her allies into the fight. On one side were Russia, France, and Britain; on the other, Germany, Austria-Hungary, and Italy. If two countries went to war and the others honored their treaty obligations, total war would break out across Europe.

In June 1914 Austrian Archduke Franz Ferdinand, the Austrian emperor's nephew and heir, made an official visit with his wife Sophie to Sarajevo in Bosnia (now a part of Yugoslavia), which had recently been annexed to the Austro-Hungarian Em-

The heir to the Austrian throne, Archduke Franz Ferdinand, and his wife are assassinated by Gavrilo Princip in Sarajevo in 1914. Princip's connection to Serbian nationalists led Austria to threaten that country; Russia, as a fellow Slavic nation, felt obliged to protect the small Balkan nation.

pire. Security was lax during the parade through the streets of Sarajevo. Only quick thinking by the driver, who gunned the accelerator, prevented disaster when someone hurled a bomb at the car. Badly shaken, the archduke demanded a different, unpublicized return route. His hosts agreed, but the driver made a wrong turn. While the driver was backing up the car, a South Slavic nationalist, Gavrilo Princip, raced from the crowd and fatally shot the archduke and his wife.

The assassination and the discovery of a conspiracy based in Serbia, a neighboring Slavic country, caused an immediate crisis in Vienna. Ironically, the archduke and his wife had been unpopular even with the emperor. But Franz Josef and his government reacted sharply to the attack on the imperial dynasty by threatening war if Serbia did not meet a list of demands within 48 hours. Austria obtained Wilhelm's unconditional support for a war

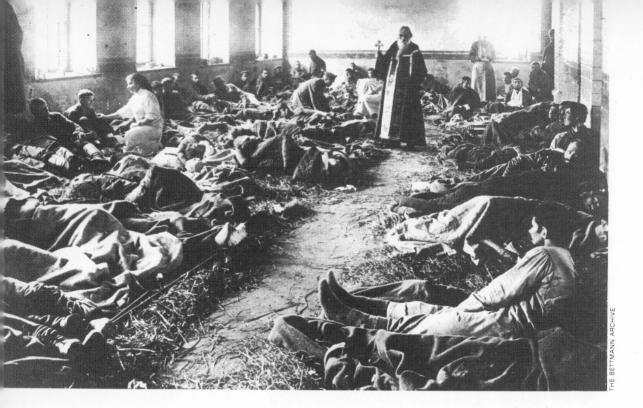

Injured soldiers crowd a church used as a Russian field hospital on the first day of the battle of Tannenberg in August 1914. The clash just inside their border was the Germans' first major victory on the eastern front.

against Serbia. Wilhelm had given Franz Josef an extensive guarantee without consulting his ministers, even though Germany could easily be drawn into an all-out war if another power decided to defend Serbia.

From Austria's declaration of war on Serbia the situation snowballed rapidly into a European war of unprecedented magnitude: World War I. Nicholas's role was crucial. The political sentiments held by the public and the government in Russia were strongly in favor of the Slavs of tiny Serbia. With the encouragement of the French ambassador in St. Petersburg, who exceeded his instructions in promising the full support of France, Nicholas and his foreign minister, Sazonov, adopted a hard line toward Austria-Hungary. They threatened to mobilize Russian forces along the two countries' common border if Austria invaded Serbia. Their confidence in taking military action had been bolstered by French President Raymond Poincaré, who already had agreed to help the Russians. It also was in the interest of France to have the German army become bogged down in a second front in the east.

Troops, guns, and supplies had to be moved into offensive positions along the borders, reserves called up, and every step up to the point of firing shots taken. To put into action and supply hundreds of thousands or even millions of troops was a huge undertaking requiring careful coordination at every step. Each European army had prepared highly secret battle plans in case of a war. It was generally expected that a war would be a brief matter, over and done within a few weeks time. The best-prepared and best-equipped armies, it was believed, would win. Therefore, no country was willing to allow an adversary the luxury of mobilizing without taking strong action in return.

Nicholas's decision to mobilize the Russian army triggered full-scale war. The elaborate Russian mobilization plan did not permit the armies to be arranged only along the Austro-Hungarian border. Russian forces massed on the German border as

> *Because of his indecisiveness Nicholas was forever attempting to prove his decisiveness — a trait which in the end brought him more swiftly to disaster than any other.*
> —HARRISON E. SALISBURY
> American historian

During World War I a Russian soldier performs a native dance to the delight of French soldiers camped at Mailly le Grand. A contingent of Russian troops had been sent to join the French near the western front.

A cartoon from the British magazine *Punch* illustrates Nicholas confronting the prospect of losing his second war in a decade.

well. Germany could not tolerate Russian troop movements menacing its border, and possibly gaining the upper hand. For the last time in their reigns, the two emperors exchanged more "Willy-Nicky" correspondence, which rapidly descended from polite concerns to Wilhelm's curt threat to declare war if Nicholas ordered mobilization. When Nicholas, after hesitating and once even retrieving the full mobilization order from the telegraph office, finally gave the order, he knew that it meant war.

Nicholas's reluctant order drew an immediate declaration of war from Germany. By declaring war on Russia, Germany pushed France to the aid of Russia, her ally. France and Germany were in a state of war. Because Great Britain's treaty obligations to France and Russia were vague it is suggested that it could have avoided immediate military involvement. But Germany struck at France by sending armies through neutral Belgium, causing terrible devastation. As a result, a morally outraged Britain joined the conflict. In less than six weeks, a group of desperate nationalists from a small country in the Balkans had caused total war in Europe. Eventually, German attacks on neutral shipping brought the United States into the conflict in 1917 on the side of Britain, France, and Russia. The "Great War" in Europe became World War I.

For Nicholas and Russia, the war began on a wave of popular support and patriotic fervor. The Duma voted war credits, which allowed the government to finance the war effort with bonds. Only the socialist members of the Duma voted against funding Russian participation in the war.

In action, the Russian armies tried to execute what they called "Plan A": simultaneous attacks on Germany and Austria, followed by a drive toward Berlin. They were hampered by a very slow mobilization that took nearly six weeks, and by strategic considerations in Poland.

Austria's war plan called for attacks against Serbia — the cause after all, of the war — and an offensive into Russian-controlled Poland south from Galicia. Using 30 divisions, Austria attacked Poland. The invading columns cut off the city of Krakow from that of Lemburg. By doing so, the Austrians hoped to disrupt the Russian mobilization near Brest-Litovsk. But the Russian army met the challenge and forced the Austrians back into and through Galicia by September. Austrian casualties totaled 300,000, as well as 40,000 lost in the Serbian campaign.

The reaction in St. Petersburg was jubilant. (During the war the city's name was changed to Petrograd, which sounded less German.) There were rash predictions of a short war and Russian victory parades in Berlin, then Germany's capital. At the same time, there were hints of crisis. Long burdened with incompetent leadership, the Russian armies were ill-clothed, undernourished, and poorly equipped. The good news turned bad very quickly.

Much of Russia's Polish territory lay sandwiched between German territory (East Prussia) to the north and Austrian territory (Galicia) to the south. To drive too quickly westward through Poland toward Berlin was to risk being encircled from behind by German and Austrian armies. The Russian generals tried to solve the problem by attacking the German forces in East Prussia with troops sent westward from Vilnius and northward from Warsaw, Poland's capital, hoping to defeat the German army in East Prussia and clear a path to Berlin.

The German forces led by General Erich Ludendorff reacted by concentrating on General Alexander Samsonov's army, which was advancing from Warsaw. In the Battle of Tannenberg from August 26 to

Guns thrown down and hands up, their leader waving a white flag, a group of Russian soldiers surrenders to the Germans in January 1915 outside Warsaw. By the end of 1914, 310,000 Russian soldiers were in German hands, including almost 4,000 officers.

August 30, 1914, the Germans routed the Russian army, taking 120,000 prisoners and capturing 350 field guns. Germany had both superior communications and transportation. The Russians were not well trained. Communications were poor between the Russian officers. When they did communicate, they carelessly sent uncoded radio messages that the Germans easily intercepted. German forces had drawn the Russian attack in one direction and then counterattacked from the opposite side. This tactic caught Samsonov's troops by surprise. Following Tannenberg, the German army wheeled and defeated the other Russian force advancing from Vilnius, taking 125,000 prisoners. The Russians had lost a quarter of a million men in casualties: a terrible price for diverting German troops from the western front and relieving some of the pressure on the French army.

When Grand Duke Nikolai Nikolaevich invaded East Prussia with a gigantic force composed of seven armies, the Russians met with another sledgehammer defeat. On November 11, German troops led by General Ludendorff and Field Marshal Paul von Hindenburg split the Russian unit in two. For the remainder of the war, the Russians would not be able to threaten Germany with invasion. In fact, by the war's end, German and Austrian forces found themselves deep within Russian territory, having advanced more than 850 miles to the city of Rostov.

The "Russian steamroller" that was commanded at the time by Grand Duke Nikolai Nikolaevich had lost its steam. When winter arrived, troops on both sides dug in and set up barricades of barbed wire. On the western front in France and Belgium, the same catastrophe was happening. From that time on, the concept of a quick war was doomed, and generals began preparing for a long, slow war of attrition, a struggle to wear down the opposing forces. Trenches, barbed wire, long-range artillery, machine guns, flame throwers, and land mines meant that the "Great War" had become a new and deadlier kind of war. To these were added airplanes and poison gas. Saber-wielding cavalry officers thundering into battle were becoming a thing of the past. No longer would such colorful gallantry characterize modern warfare. Fortified lines, bristling with barbed wire and machine guns, would face one another across bleak battlefields commonly called "no man's land."

Russia, more than any other combatant, had gambled on a short war. At the outset, there was less than a week's supply of ammunition readily available. On only the fourth day of the war, one general sent an urgent telegram to the minister of war complaining of a shortage of ammunition and requesting more. The 5.6 million rifles that were supposed to be in the government arsenals existed mainly on paper, probably the result of prewar corruption in various governmental departments. Unlike the Germans, the Russians also lacked both light and heavy artillery. As the war dragged on, their supplies began to fall short and troops were rationed bullets, as well as food. Some soldiers were court-martialed for firing more than their quota of two or three shells per day. Some were forced to go into combat using only bayonets because there were no bullets for the rifles, and some had no rifles on

Among the nurses tending Russian casualties at the Tsarskoe Selo hospital are (from left) Grand Duchesses Olga and Tatiana, and Tsarina Alexandra. The tsarina and her daughters spent a great deal of time doing volunteer work for the wounded during World War I.

which to attach their bayonets.

Four months into the war, Nicholas wrote to Alexandra that because of ammunition shortages "our troops have to observe economy and discretion during action, which means that the brunt of the fighting falls upon the infantry. Owing to that, the losses at once become colossal. . . . Reinforcements are coming in well, but half of them have no rifles, as the troops are losing masses. There is nobody to collect them on the battlefields."

After the long winter, Germany and Austria opened a counterattack that forced the Russians from Galicia, Russian Poland, and territory that had been Russian-held since the 1770s. By August, the war had cost Russia 1.5 million killed or wounded and 1.5 million taken prisoner. The British military observer in Russia estimated that the entire Russian army at the beginning of winter in 1915 had only 650,000 rifles, 2,590 machine guns, and 4,000 small field pieces. In practical terms, it meant that Russia could not defend the vast German-Austrian front with armed men.

Russia soon could not supply the army with weapons, nor could she feed it. The planners and transportation officials could not, or would not, move grain and other vital provisions from the farmlands to the front. Some feared peasant revolts if the government took any more food from the countryside.

Meanwhile, another "steamroller," this time a German one led by General August von Mackensen, forced the Russians from Poland by defeating them at Gorlice in 1915. Mackensen was known for expertly using massed artillery bombardments against the Russian fortifications, wiping out their defenders. The German infantry, "creeping like some huge beast," as one Russian general described it, "would stretch out its paws" and seize the enemy trenches. Poorly armed and inexperienced Russian recruits were no match for such a technologically superior opponent. By the fall of 1915 Russia was losing the war of logistics (supply and equipment maintenance) and was on the verge of complete military collapse.

Nicholas made a fateful decision that August.

Nicholas (right) confers with his uncle, Grand Duke Nikolai Nikolaevich, commander in chief of the Russian armed forces. Nicholas dismissed the grand duke in August 1915 and took command himself.

THE BETTMANN ARCHIVE

Alexandra wears her uniform as head of the Lancer's Regiment. A member of the regiment would later make an unsuccessful attempt to free the imperial family from house arrest after Nicholas's abdication.

Once before, in the darkest hours of the Russo-Japanese War, Nicholas had decided to assume personal command of his failing armed forces. At that time his family and advisers were able to dissuade him. In 1915, ignoring the protests of 10 of his ministers, Nicholas removed Grand Duke Nikolai Nikolaevich as commander in chief, went off to his personal headquarters, and assumed the high command himself. A poor organizer and a worse strategist, Nicholas was soon bogged down in the endless detail of military campaigns. As tsar, he could rise above defeat in the eyes of his subjects; as commander in chief, he was responsible for them. As the military duties consumed more and more of his time, he deputized Alexandra to oversee the affairs of government. Within a week of Nicholas's departure for the headquarters of the commander in chief, Alexandra once again began exerting her dangerously misguided influence over the affairs of state.

The European war has brought this great benefit to international socialism, that it has exposed for all to see the utter rottenness, baseness, and meanness of opportunism, thereby giving a splendid impetus to the cleansing of the working-class movement from the dung accumulated during decades of peace.
—VLADIMIR LENIN
Russian communist leader

83

6

The Tsarina and Rasputin

Nicholas's major and ultimately fatal flaw as a leader was his lack of sound judgment about close associates and family friends. In part, the tsar allowed his heart to rule his head, for he found it difficult to find fault with anyone — particularly anyone liked by his beloved Sunny. On the whole, the tsar was himself a poor judge of character. Nicholas was essentially nostalgic toward the role of tsar. He looked back to the grandeur of the Muscovite era and the age of Peter the Great, who was the architect of tsarist absolutism in the late 17th and early 18th centuries. But it was not Peter, but Alexei Mikhailovich, Peter's father, after whom Nicholas was expected to model himself. Alexei was a charming, somewhat sensual man who also impressed his courtiers and his subjects with his love of religious piety. His interests were far-ranging and included a passion for scientific discovery. His progressive views were a prelude to Peter the Great's even greater devotion to modernization. Nicholas fell far short of both these extraordinary rulers. Too often he elevated bad managers to high office simply because

I breathe easily only when you, my teacher, sit beside me and I kiss your hand and put my head on your holy shoulder.
—ALEXANDRA
from a letter to Rasputin

A Russian cartoon shows the mystic Gregory Rasputin as the power behind the throne. Nicholas so indulged his wife, who was in Rasputin's thrall, that he would not move against the man who even further alienated the populace, including the nobles, from the royal family.

Alexei Mikhailovich was tsar from 1645 to 1676 and fathered Peter the Great. Like Peter, he was a man of intellectual breadth and curiosity, but he also respected religious authority. Nicholas was expected to model himself after these tsars.

he felt comfortable with their ultra-conservative views or because someone he trusted had recommended them. Instead of seeking a broad range of advice, particularly as important decisions loomed, Nicholas surrounded himself with flatterers, reactionary cranks, and worse. In this he was encouraged by his wife, whose appetite for meddling in affairs of state would play a major role in the family's tragic fate.

Alexandra and Nicholas's personal tragedy began with the long-awaited birth of a male heir to the throne in 1904. After four daughters, none of whom could inherit the throne, the cannons at last sounded 300 times to announce the birth of a tsarevich. For a week, all was well, but on the eighth day young Alexis began bleeding uncontrollably from the navel. After frantic consultations, the doctors delivered their verdict: hemophilia, an inherited disease characterized by the blood's inability to clot, or coagulate. Later studies showed that Queen Victoria of England had passed the flawed gene to most of the royal houses of Europe through royal marriages of her daughters. The recessive gene that causes the disease is carried by females but the condition almost always occurs in males. One of Victoria's own sons, and the heir to the Spanish throne, died of Victoria's transmitted hemophilia.

The heir to the Russian throne clearly faced an uncertain future. Even a routine bump or bruise could be fatal if the internal bleeding were not somehow stopped. Today the disease is controlled, not cured, by transfusions of donor blood plasma containing the missing clotting factor. In 1904 very little was known about the disease except that it was genetically transmitted by females.

For the imperial couple, the news was shattering. In a panic, they swore to secrecy everyone who knew. Though the tsarevich was known to be in "delicate condition," few persons outside the immediate family and medical staff knew the whole truth. Even Pierre Gilliard, the tutor to the tsar's children, did not learn the real reason for Alexis's sudden absences for almost eight years.

Alexandra threw herself into the care and security of the future tsar. She rarely ventured beyond the immediate family, associating with almost none of the tsar's many relatives, and relied increasingly on often lackluster court hangers-on, medical quacks, and "holy men" for company and guidance. Alexandra's chief confidante and companion was Anna Vyrubova, a plump, dull woman of good family who said the right things, and soon became a permanent fixture of the imperial household. As the tsarina's circle narrowed, so did the tsar's.

Like many of her contemporaries, Alexandra was drawn toward religious mysticism, miracle workers, and strange and wonderful cures for almost everything. Before Alexis's birth, she had employed several characters to cure illnesses or guarantee a male heir. Burdened with guilt and the terrible secret of

> *A starets takes your soul, your will, into his soul and his will. In choosing a starets, you renounce any will of your own, and you surrender it to him in complete obedience and with total self-abnegation.*
> —FYODOR DOSTOEVSKY
> Russian writer, from
> *The Brothers Karamazov*

Alexis, heir to the Russian throne, sat for this painting just before World War I. He was born with hemophilia, which at the time was an untreatable disease.

An unforgettable day for us in which God clearly showed us his blessing. At 1:15 p.m. Alix gave birth to a son whom with a prayer we have named Alexis.

—NICHOLAS II
from his diary entry for
July 30, 1904

Alexis's disease, the tsarina was quick to listen to anyone who professed to ease or cure the tsarevich's hemophilia. And Gregory Rasputin seemed to do exactly that.

Born Gregory Yefimovich, the young Siberian peasant was called Rasputin (probably from *rasputnik* or "libertine") by his fellow villagers in testimony to his habit of getting his way with women. Rasputin did marry and raise a family of daughters before feeling the religious impulse and becoming a *starets*, or holy man. The true starets was usually a hermit-like old man, revered for his religious devotion, or a pilgrim who renounced worldly interests, including sex, and wandered the empire preaching to those who would listen. Rasputin fit neither of these descriptions, leading most historians to conclude that he was a fraud — a crafty, immoral ruffian who exploited bored, idle women.

Rasputin was physically impressive, very muscular with broad shoulders. Acquaintances from cabinet ministers to society matrons often remarked on his intense, narrow-set, steely gray eyes, which seemed to burn with strange powers. From descriptions of his treatments, it seems likely that Rasputin practiced some form of hypnotism, or mesmerism as it was called during the 18th and 19th centuries. He cultivated his simple peasant origins, which both shocked and disarmed Russian society. He dressed in country garb, had an unkempt beard, dirty nails, and greasy hair, spoke coarsely, often profanely, and smelled like a goat. Having somehow gained the blessing of a few high Orthodox churchmen, Rasputin became a sensation in St. Petersburg society. In 1905 he met the tsar and tsarina at Tsarskoe Selo for the first time, and his star began to rise.

The turning point in his relationship with the imperial family was Alexis's accident at Spala, the family's Polish hunting lodge. The tsarevich fell against an oarlock in a boat and bruised himself severely. As the internal bleeding this accident caused continued, the blood formed a huge hematoma (a blister-like swelling) over much of his leg and abdomen. The pain was excruciating and the internal loss of blood nearly fatal. A priest admin-

Alexis takes a trip in 1914 on the imperial yacht _Standart_ in the company of Pierre Gilliard, tutor to the tsar's children.

istered last rites, and several times it appeared that any breath might be Alexis's last. The desperate Alexandra telegraphed Rasputin, who sent a return cable saying that the doctors should not disturb Alexis too much and that he would recover. Miraculously, or so it seemed to Alexandra, he did. From that time on, Rasputin's healing abilities were an article of faith for Alexandra. On several later occasions, Rasputin did, in fact, seem to stop Alexis's bleeding spells with a combination of relaxed storytelling and hypnosis. When Anna Vyrubova suffered a very severe accident, Rasputin accurately predicted that she would survive but would be permanently crippled. The tsarina's letters were soon full of glowing references to "Our Friend."

To Count Vladimir Kokovtsev, Peter Stolypin's successor as the tsar's prime minister, Rasputin was little more than a "Siberian convict." Nicholas was nevertheless impressed by this peasant who

A Russian silver-gilt icon triptych dating from about 1890 shows, from left, Saint Alexander Nevsky, Christ Pantocrator, and Saint Demetrius. Devastated by her son's illness, Alexandra turned increasingly to religion to provide a cure.

seemed both saint and medicine man.

By 1911 Rasputin was firmly entrenched in St. Petersburg and the affections of the imperial family. At his modest quarters in Gorokhavaya Street, he held court, offering spiritual guidance, peddling his influence with the tsar's ministers, and taking much of his payment in sexual favors. His technique was simple: as a man of God, he offered spiritual forgiveness of sins and eternal salvation. As Rasputin's influence grew, so did his boldness. Numerous women filed attempted rape charges against him, but the police were powerless against the well-connected starets. Church leaders accused him of attempting to seduce and rape a nun, and he admitted it. But those who crossed him or denounced him, including a high police official and his disillusioned church sponsors, soon found themselves retired or shipped off to duties in the provinces.

Alarmed by Rasputin's easy access to the imperial family, Prime Minister Stolypin once gave Nicholas a full report on Rasputin's activities. Nicholas replied, "Perhaps everything you say is true. But I must ask you never to speak to me again about Rasputin. In any case, I can do nothing about it." Nicholas was admitting that he could not bring himself to deny his wife the holy man who she thought had saved their son.

Meanwhile, Rasputin was becoming more notorious by the day. Ugly rumors — none ever proved — spread concerning his relationship with the tsarina and her daughters. Knowing Rasputin, people were only too willing to believe the worst. Alexandra, never popular with the nobility, became less so. Her response to those who tried to tell her the truth about Rasputin's "love" affairs was to reply that even the Apostles had kissed each other as a greeting. Eventually, she turned against anyone who spoke ill of Rasputin and, in actions typical of someone suffering from paranoia, came to view everyone as either friend or enemy. Gradually, the list of friends shortened and the list of enemies grew.

After the outbreak of war in 1914, Nicholas spent more and more time at military headquarters near the front and less time dealing with matters of gov-

THE BETTMANN ARCHIVE

Rasputin gained the protection of the throne for his numerous misdeeds because Alexandra thought he had mystical powers to preserve the delicate Alexis from harm. He became a liability for the tsar after 1912, when he was attacked in the press and the Duma.

ernment. Alexandra Fyodorovna kept up a steady flow of letters — more than 400 between 1914 and 1916 — in which she referred constantly to "Our Friend" and passed along Rasputin's suggestions for everything from the civilian food supply to military tactics. Nicholas treasured her warm, loving letters, which were usually filled with details of family life, and often (but not always) took "Our Friend's" advice.

With his assumption of supreme command of the army, Nicholas in effect turned over the civil government to Alexandra, which ultimately led to Rasputin having a much increased say in ruling the nation. The combination proved extremely dangerous to the Russian imperial state — especially when threatened with possible military defeat. A hint of disapproval from Rasputin was enough to doom a ministerial career. For her part, Alexandra approved and recommended appointment of only those ministers who shared her dream of saving tsarist autocracy for the young tsarevich and who were able to get along with Rasputin. Alexandra and Rasputin were instrumental in the dismissal of, first, Grand Duke Nikolai Nikolaevich as supreme commander, then the very able war minister, and also the interior minister, among others. They succeeded in elevating the well-meaning but unstatesmanlike Boris V. Stürmer to the office of prime minister in February 1916. Of the new prime minister, the French ambassador wrote, "His appointment becomes intelligible on the supposition that he has been selected solely as a tool; in other words, actually on account of his insignificance and servility. . . . [He] has been warmly recommended to the emperor by Rasputin." His appointment to foreign minister a few months later was considered a farce.

As the Russian war effort continued to crumble, Rasputin toyed with the inner workings of the state, appointing three ministers of war and four ministers of agriculture in one year. In fact, it had been Rasputin who had pressed Nicholas to take personal command of the Russian military. Rasputin's scandalous behavior continued unchecked. Often drunk in public, the "holy man" was known to have made

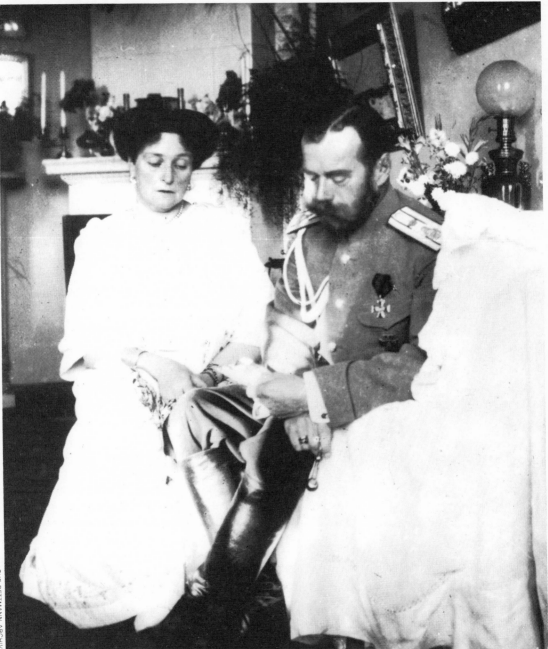

Nicholas and Alexandra read a message in October 1912 at their hunting lodge at Spala. They were keeping vigil over Alexis, who nearly died after internal bleeding caused by a fall. Rasputin became unshakably lodged in Alexandra's favor when he predicted Alexis's recovery.

advances to horrified women at social gatherings. His apartment was the site of so many "consultations" and "salvations" that the police reports kept by the officers who were there to protect Rasputin and control the crush of visitors were passed around St. Petersburg. Member after member of the imperial family tried to make Alexandra understand the truth, but even her beloved sister was dismissed "like a dog." When ministers or family members sent critical reports directly to Nicholas, he passed them to Alexandra, who merely added more names to her list of "Our Friend's" enemies.

Finally, with the reputation and fate of the imperial family in jeopardy, an unlikely group took action. The chief was Prince Felix Yusupov, the 29-year-old heir to Russia's greatest fortune. He joined forces with an outraged conservative member of the Duma, an army officer, a doctor, and Nicholas's cousin, the 26-year-old Grand Duke Dmitri Pavlovich. Together, they plotted Rasputin's assassination.

Using a supposed rendezvous with Prince Felix's beautiful wife as bait, the conspirators lured Rasputin to Yusupov's palace one evening in December 1916. There, they fed him enough poisoned teacakes and madeira (which he preferred to vodka) to kill a crowd. When the cyanide only made Rasputin groggy, Yusupov shot him in the chest with a revolver, and the doctor pronounced him dead. Then, as the prince recalled in his memoirs, the starets suddenly lurched back to life, attacked Yusupov, and staggered from the palace. Several more shots finally brought him crashing down in the snow. They then bound the body with rope and heaved it through a hole in the ice of the Neva River. The police, finding a carelessly discarded shoe on the ice, discovered the body. While no official autopsy was permitted by the tsar, police reports show that the man had died not of poisoning, not of his gunshot wounds, which probably were slight — but of drowning. Among government officials and the nobility, the conspirators, who were quickly identified, were heroes. Unable or unwilling to take severe action, Nicholas banished Yusupov to one of his many country estates, sent Grand Duke Dmitri to the war

Prince Felix Yusupov led Rasputin's assassins. They were looked upon as heroes for their deed. Yusupov's only punishment was to be banished to his comfortable estate outside Moscow.

front in Persia, where he survived both the war and the revolution, and took no action whatever against the popular Duma member. Alexandra and Nicholas both attended Rasputin's burial at Tsarskoe Selo.

Rasputin's influence on Russian history extended well beyond the scandals and the degradation of the imperial family. He and Alexandra, working always through the arm of Nicholas's orders, paralyzed civil government through their misguided purges and woefully ill-qualified appointees. At a time when the war news was bleak and food shortages were becoming severe, government simply ceased to function, thus triggering events that would finish the monarchy and the imperial family.

7

The End of a Dynasty

Not only was Alexei Putilov Russia's great munitions manufacturer, but he seems to have been something of a prophet. Putilov told the French ambassador in mid-1915, "the Days of Tsarism are numbered. . . . Revolution is now inevitable. It is only waiting for a favorable opportunity. Such an opportunity will come with some military defeat, a famine in the provinces, a strike in Petrograd, a riot in Moscow, some scandal or tragedy at the palace. . . . From the bourgeois revolution, we shall at once descend to the working class revolution, and soon after to the peasant revolution."

After Rasputin's assassination Nicholas returned for a time to Tsarskoe Selo and all but ceased to govern. Around him lay economic and military chaos. Bread cost three times as much as it had in 1914, beef five-and-a-half times, and potatoes eight times as much. Rents had doubled and tripled, but wages had barely risen. Public services were breaking down. Strikes had broken out at numerous factories and the military appeared disinterested. The winter of 1916–17 was so severe that boiler pipes in train locomotives froze and burst, causing some

Nothing save the victory of the proletariat will be able to rid the world of hatred.
—MAXIM GORKY
Russian novelist
and playwright

Having abdicated his throne, an ailing Nicholas sits in a wheelchair in July 1918 at Ekaterinburg, in the Ural Mountains, a few days before his Bolshevik guards murdered him and his family.

A painting commemorates the role of workers and sailors in the revolutions of 1917. The rebellion began in March with a spontaneous uprising of workers in Petrograd, followed by the mutiny of soldiers posted there and sailors stationed at the nearby Kronstadt base.

SOVFOTO

60,000 boxcars of food and fuel to be stranded and gradually buried under huge snowdrifts. By January 1917 Petrograd was suffering severe food and fuel shortages.

Members of the imperial family tried without success to impress upon Nicholas and Alexandra the seriousness of their position. One grand duke tried to convince Alexandra that Nicholas should appoint a cabinet of ministers acceptable and responsible to the Duma. She was outraged. "Nicky is an autocrat," she replied. "How could he share his divine rights with a parliament?" To the last, Alexandra denied that the October 1905 revolution had ever taken place.

Visitors to Tsarskoe Selo during this period were horrified at the change in the tsar. In a year's time, he had aged decades. His eyes were dull and yellow, his face lined and wrinkled, his cheeks hollow. Count Kokovtsev, on one occasion, said the tsar listened to him with a "sick smile" and "kept glancing from side to side in a strange way." He left convinced that the tsar was suffering a nervous breakdown. Gripped by depression and bewildered by the chaos that had descended on Russia, the tsar might have begun using drugs, such as cocaine and opium.

Elected in the fall of 1912, the Fourth Duma did not actually convene until August 1915. Only a few months earlier, the Russian army, reeling from its

A drawing by N. Patslov depicts a demonstration attended by factory workers in Petrograd in 1917.

defeat at Gorlice in Poland, had begun retreating in confusion. Moderate elements in the Duma were collapsing. The Octobrists, for example, had opposed the government on many issues. Yet they had tried to avoid giving in to extremists. When Nicholas refused to recognize unofficial governments, such as the workers' soviets, however, the Octobrists were forced to join with the reform-minded Progressive party. When this majority offered Nicholas a plan to form a coalition government and a new cabinet, the tsar's ministers told him to disband the Duma. This was done in September 1915. As the war and civil unrest were causing the old Russian autocracy to come crashing down around Nicholas, he still could not grasp the urgent need to change course. Without cooperation between the tsar and an elected assembly, the Russian people turned to their last, painful choice: revolution.

When the Duma met again in 1916, Prime Minister Goremykin was forced to resign. Neither his successor, Stürmer, nor the foreign minister, Dmitri Trepov, could address the legislature. They were booed and shouted down. One of Nicholas's generals did succeed in telling the Duma that the war situation was worse than ever: "A revolution is imminent and we at the front feel it to be so." As the streets of Petrograd erupted in violence, the Duma was again broken up on March 11, 1917 (February 26, according to the old calendar). The next day, the Russian people and the imperial family awoke to what became known as the February Revolution.

At first confined to small demonstrations in the working class quarters of Petrograd, the crowds swelled as they were joined by striking steel workers and women who had been turned away empty-handed from bread lines. On Friday, the crowds formed again, perhaps 200,000 people in all, shouting, "Down with autocracy!" and "Down with war!" and "Give us bread!" This time, they moved into the center of the city, joking with the soldiers who were supposed to control them, and avoiding wherever possible the tough tsarist police. On Saturday, an even larger crowd gathered, this time chanting, "Down with the Tsar!"

Nicholas had returned to the military front and was receiving regular bulletins, not about the uprising but about his daughters, who were falling ill with measles. Only on Saturday did he learn of the disorders in Petrograd. Later that day he sent a telegram to the Petrograd commandant: "I order you to bring all of these disorders in the capital to a halt as of tomorrow. These cannot be permitted in this difficult time of war with Germany and Austria." Nicholas had no idea of the changing mood of the people or the difficulty of restoring order. The commandant was stunned, for the order left him no alternative but to use force. He instructed his men to give three warnings to disperse groups and then to shoot if necessary.

On Sunday, crowds again gathered. They were

A crowd of workers who pushed past barriers into Nevsky Prospekt, Petrograd's major boulevard, flees as soldiers fire into the throng on Sunday, March 11, 1917. Nicholas had ordered the commander of the Petrograd garrison to use force.

On April 27, 1917, soldiers in Petrograd kneel on the running board of a car, displaying their allegiance to the soviet by the red flags draped over their guns. The Petrograd Soviet was a rival for power of the Provisional Government, which worked with the Duma.

warned to leave three times. Then the order was given to open fire. Most of the soldiers fired into the air, refusing to shoot the workers. Some soldiers were forced by furious officers to take aim and fire, and several demonstrators were killed before the crowd broke up. But later the same day, a military regiment fired on the tsarist police instead of the workers. Other regiments soon joined in.

Leaders of the Duma frantically telegraphed the tsar, asking him to appoint a new cabinet to work with them in restoring order. Nicholas ignored their appeals and spent several hours playing dominoes.

By Monday, the workers and the Petrograd garrison of soldiers had seized control of the city. On March 11, still unaware of the seriousness of the situation, Nicholas left his headquarters to make the long train trip to Tsarskoe Selo. During the journey he was forced to take a detour at the city of Pskov. Once there, he was informed by General Nikolai Ruzsky, who reported on conversations with leaders of the Duma, that the situation in Petrograd was critical and that using force was useless. The tsar's capital and the routes into it were in the hands of the revolutionaries. The only solution was for Nicholas to abdicate the throne in the hope of saving the dynasty.

Unable to bear the thought of separating himself and his wife from the ailing tsarevich, Nicholas chose to abdicate and be succeeded by his brother, Grand Duke Mikhail Alexandrovich. The grand duke, however, wisely refused the crown unless it was offered by a popularly elected assembly.

On March 15 (March 2, according to the old calendar), Nicholas calmly and matter-of-factly signed his short abdication statement. With that act, the 304-year-old Romanov imperial dynasty came to an abrupt end. Without a successor to the throne and

Thousands of soldiers and civilians listen to a Bolshevik orator in Petrograd in front of the Winter Palace in 1917. They are protected by the Red Guards, a workers' militia controlled by the city's soviet, which was organized by the socialists in early March.

Nicholas II assumed a normal condition for Russia in which a tranquil people were loyal to an absolute monarch, and any temporary abnormality was taken to be the work of "troublemakers."
—DONALD W. TREADGOLD
American historian

The Bettmann Archive

Nicholas shovels snow in 1917 at Tsarskoe Selo, where he was kept under guard with his family. No longer allowed the run of the palace, the family had access to only part of it and a section of the grounds.

with no other ruling body then in existence, observers were surprised at his self-control. Only in his diary did Nicholas confide his bitterness at the "treason, cowardice, and deceit" that he saw around him. Alexandra, upon learning the news of the abdication, wept uncontrollably.

In early March, the new Provisional Government of leading figures in the Duma permitted Nicholas to rejoin his family at Tsarskoe Selo. At the gates to the Alexander Palace, without ceremony, a sentry simply identified the occupant of the car as "Nicholas Romanov." The following months were a time of great uncertainty as factions within the government argued over the fate of the unpopular former tsar and tsarina. Some wanted a public trial, and others wished to engineer a quick exile to England. Gradually, the Alexander Palace became an elegant prison, but with large portions of the building and grounds forbidden to the family. To while away the time, Nicholas shoveled snow, and led the children in planting a vegetable garden.

Shortly before his return to Russia from exile in April 1917, Lenin announced in Zürich, Switzerland, what the Bolsheviks should do: "Our tactics — absolute distrust, no support for the provisional government. Distrust Kerensky above all . . . ." Alexander Kerensky had been a prominent member of the Fourth Duma since 1912. He began his political career as a brilliant young lawyer who successfully defended revolutionaries against prosecution during the days of Nicholas and Stolypin's crackdown on unrest. Himself a radical, Kerensky had been a member of the Social Revolutionary party, one of the Bolsheviks' rivals. Kerensky openly insisted on the tsar's abdication, and became the minister of justice for the Provisional Government that was formed when the tsar gave in to the demand. He somehow managed at the same time to hold a leading seat in the Petrograd Soviet. He had one foot in the Provisional Government and one in an ongoing revolution, which the Bolsheviks were determined to lead. In May 1917 he became the Provisional Government's leader. The previous prime minister, Prince Georgy Lvov, a landowning noble who was a leading figure in the zemstvo and in the Kadet party, was widely seen as too conservative. In July Lvov resigned from the cabinet, having lost all influence on government decisions.

In Petrograd, however, the Provisional Government itself was falling victim to increasingly radical elements. To safeguard the Romanov family, worried leaders decided to move them in great secrecy away from radical Petrograd to quieter surroundings in western Siberia. Their destination lay three days away by rail and a long boat ride. Fearful that radical workers would attack the train if they learned of its human cargo, the Provisional Government disguised it as a Japanese Red Cross mission and sent Nicholas, his family, servants, pets, and baggage safely to Tobolsk. There, they lived very comfortably in the provincial governor's house through the fall, winter, and spring.

However, the Provisional Government was soon overthrown by radical Bolsheviks led by Lenin in November 1917. While Kerensky was away at the front trying to muster troops to combat the revolution, the well-organized Bolsheviks quietly took

Soldiers in a Petrograd street burn the royal insignia removed from shops and buildings in 1917.

Workers guard their prize, an armored car captured from the troops of the Provisional Government during the Bolshevik revolution in November 1917.

over everything of strategic importance in Petrograd. With banks, transportation, and communications firmly in their control, they closed in on the Winter Palace. Once Nicholas's residence, it housed the Provisional Government and its ministers. Without bloodshed Bolshevik-led soldiers captured the palace that had been Kerensky's headquarters. The Bolshevik triumph (often called the October Revolution from its old calender date) touched off a competition among various groups within the movement for custody of the imperial prisoners. In this tense atmosphere, all eyes turned toward Lenin's government, which had moved to Moscow. Among the promises he made was to end Russia's involvement in World War I, one of the root causes of Nicholas's downfall. Lenin would send Trotsky to Brest-Litovsk, Poland, in the winter of 1918 to negotiate a settlement with Germany and Austria. Meanwhile, a brutal civil war had already broken out in Russia between the "Reds," as the communists were called, and their opponents, termed the "Whites."

The tug-of-war for custody of the Romanovs was won by the most radical elements. In late April 1918 the family was moved to a grand private house in Ekaterinburg and placed under the control of the Regional Soviet of the Urals. The guards permitted them no privacy and few of the comforts to which they had been accustomed.

> *Nicholas thought that he had been forced to give Russians too much too soon. In fact, he had given them too little too late.*
> —W. BRUCE LINCOLN
> American historian

SOVFOTO

Ragtag Red Guards muster in 1917. They equipped themselves with whatever they could find.

In Moscow, Lenin's Ministry of Justice was beginning to assemble evidence for a public trial of the former tsar and tsarina when other events forced a change of plan. Russia was in the grip of civil war, the pro-Bolshevik Reds fighting the anti-communist (and very often pro-tsarist) Whites. In the spring of 1918 the White Army scored several major victories along the Trans-Siberian Railway and began moving steadily toward Ekaterinburg.

With White Army rescuers only days away from the Romanovs, Lenin either permitted the Regional Soviet to take action against the imperial family, or gave the order directly himself. No one knows quite how it happened, but the result was an order to Yakov Yurovsky, local chief of the Bolshevik secret police, to prevent any rescue by executing the imperial family and their attendants.

Yurovsky planned efficiently. He ordered barrels of sulfuric acid and gasoline delivered to the Four Brothers Mine outside Ekaterinburg. He chose his men and carefully instructed them. At 2:00 A.M. on July 18 the soldiers awakened their prisoners, telling them to dress and prepare for a rapid evacuation to avoid the advancing White Army. The family and

Cossack cavalry goes on the march. With a long history of opposition to the central government, the Cossacks formed an autonomous regime and took up arms against the Bolsheviks in the civil war that began in 1917.

UPI BETTMANN NEWSPHOTOS

Cannon guard the Smolny Institute in Petrograd in November 1917. Once a school for girls of the nobility, it now became the temporary headquarters of the new Bolshevik government.

servants were seated in a small ground-floor room to await transportation.

With a truck engine providing background noise, Yurovsky marched his soldiers into the room and announced to a startled Nicholas that, by order of the Regional Soviet, he and his family were to be shot. Nicholas leaped up and barely uttered the word "What?" before Yurovsky killed him with a pistol shot to the head. Yurovsky and his men immediately opened fire on the rest of the family and attendants, some of whom died making the sign of the cross. In the hail of pistol fire, Anastasia was only slightly wounded, so the soldiers killed her with bayonets.

Working methodically, the soldiers loaded the bodies into the waiting truck and drove to the mine. They cut the bodies into pieces, poured gasoline over the remains, and burned them. Afterward they poured acid over unburned pieces of bone and unceremoniously tossed what was left of the Romanovs and their servants down the mine shaft.

A week later, the rescuing army arrived in Ekaterinburg and went straight to the house where the family had been held. They found only Alexis's pet dog, half-starving but alive. Eventually investigators

Alexandra busies herself
with needlepoint at Tsarskoe
Selo after Nicholas's abdication in 1917.

friendly to the imperial family discovered the burial
site and found what remained of the Romanovs:
various rings, some corset stays, one well-mani-
cured finger tip, and a small collection of miscella-
neous junk that Pierre Gilliard, the children's tutor,
sadly identified as the usual contents of young
Alexis's pocket.

Hostage-taking was used by the Bolsheviks
against their enemies. The hostages' captors would
not hesitate to kill them. As the Russian civil war
raged, and the communists and noncommunists
fought over their nation's future, Prince Kropotkin,
the anarchist, wrote Lenin a letter, asking if he realized that such methods returned Russia "to the
worst time of the Middle Ages. . . ." Kropotkin demanded, "Is there really no one amongst you who
understands what a hostage is?"

The fate of the Romanovs prompted many rumors
and legends. In later years, a woman appeared in
Germany claiming then and for decades after to be
Anastasia. The courts and surviving relatives con-

cluded that she was not, but the notion that one of the tsar's children had survived was an idea that would not go away. Similarly, tales of a huge fortune in the Bank of England awaiting the rightful heir to the throne were false but hard to put down.

In fact, many of Nicholas's relatives did escape Russia in time and spent the rest of their years in European or Canadian exile. Two of the tsar's sisters lived until 1960, one dying in an apartment over a barbershop in East Toronto, Canada. His mother, the dowager empress, returned to her native Denmark to live in a wing of the Danish royal palace. Others escaped too, including the ballerina Kschessinska, who later married Grand Duke Andrei. And Prince Felix Yusupov, the man who killed Rasputin, escaped with his wife, Princess Irina, into wealthy exile in France to became a mainstay of the little community of emigrés who once had formed the Russian monarchy.

From left, Olga, Alexis, Anastasia, and Tatiana relax on the lawn of one of their temporary homes in 1918. Although rumors of Anastasia's escape from execution abounded, emigré members of the royal family have always believed she died with her family in July 1918.

Further Reading

Gilliard, Pierre. *Thirteen Years at the Russian Court.* New York: Arno Press, 1970.

Lafore, Laurence. *The Long Fuse.* Philadelphia: Lippincott, 1965.

Lincoln, W. Bruce. *The Romanovs: Autocrats of All the Russias.* New York: Dial Press, 1981.

Massie, Robert K. *Nicholas and Alexandra.* New York: Atheneum, 1967.

Riasanovsky, Nicholas. *A History of Russia.* New York: Oxford University Press, 1984.

Salisbury, Harrison E. *Black Night, White Snow: Russia's Revolutions 1905–1917.* Garden City, NY: Doubleday & Co., Inc., 1978.

Treadgold, Donald. *Twentieth-Century Russia.* Boston: Houghton Mifflin, 1962.

Tuchman, Barbara. *The Guns of August.* New York: Macmillan, 1962.

Walder, David. *The Short Victorious War: The Russo-Japanese Conflict, 1904–1905.* New York: Harper & Row, 1973.

Chronology

May 18, 1868	Born Nicholas Romanov
March 13, 1881	Nicholas' grandfather, Tsar Alexander II, is assassinated by revolutionaries
Nov. 1894	Death of Nicholas' father, Tsar Alexander III; Nicholas becomes tsar
	Nicholas marries Alix of Hesse-Darmstadt, who takes the name Alexandra Fyodorovna
May 27, 1896	Over a thousand Russians celebrating Nicholas and Alexandra's coronation are trampled to death at Khodynka Field
1900	Russia occupies Manchuria
1902	Leo Tolstoy warns Nicholas that revolution is imminent unless reforms are passed
1904–05	Russo-Japanese War
Jan. 22, 1905	Hundreds of workers petitioning the tsar are killed or wounded by soldiers in the Bloody Sunday massacre
Oct. 1905	A massive general strike paralyzes Russia
Oct. 30, 1905	Nicholas issues the October Manifesto, creating a constitutional monarchy and a popularly elected legislature, the *Duma*
June 28, 1914	Archduke Franz Ferdinand, the nephew of the Austrian emperor, is shot, leading to the outbreak of World War I
Aug. 1, 1914	Germany declares war on Russia
Sept. 5, 1915	Nicholas takes command of the Russian armies
Dec. 30, 1916	Gregory Rasputin is assassinated
March 1917	Strikes and riots break out in Petrograd; workers and soldiers seize control of the city
March 15, 1917	Nicholas abdicates the throne; Russia is governed by a Provisional Government made up of representatives from the Duma
Aug. 14, 1917	Nicholas and his family are sent to Tobolsk, Siberia
Nov. 7, 1917	Lenin and the Bolsheviks come to power
April 1918	The Romanovs are moved to Ekaterinburg by the Bolsheviks
July 18, 1918	The Romanovs are shot by Bolshevik soldiers in Ekaterinburg

Index

George Vogt is Director of the Records Program at the National Historical Publication and Records Commission in Washington, D.C. He received his Ph.D. in history at the University of Virginia, and has published several articles in the field of American history.

Arthur M. Schlesinger, jr., taught history at Harvard for many years and is currently Albert Schweitzer Professor of the Humanities at City University of New York. He is the author of numerous highly praised works in American history and has twice been awarded the Pulitzer Prize. He served in the White House as special assistant to Presidents Kennedy and Johnson.